Perceptions About Reality Through Simulations by Software

Marcos Tewfiq holds bachelor's degrees in Electronics Engineering (from Instituto Tecnológico de Aeronáutica - ITA, in Brazil), Law, and Economics (both from the Pontifical Catholic University of Rio Grande do Sul - PUCRS, in Brazil). His attention to technology leads him to continuous education, for example, through online courses. Therefore, it is worth mentioning some online courses related to the subject of this book: C++ Nanodegree Program, by Udacity; Professional Certificate in C Programming with Linux, by Dartmouth College and Institut Mines-Télécom, on edX; 2.086x: Computational Thinking for Modeling and Simulation, by MITx, on edX. In addition, although indirectly related to the book, deserve to be mentioned these courses on Coursera: Fundamentals of Computing Specialization, by Rice University; Intro to Robotics Specialization, by the University of Pennsylvania; Cybersecurity Specialization, by the University of Maryland; Power Electronics Specialization, by the University of Colorado Boulder; An Introduction to Programming the Internet of Things (IoT) Specialization, by the University of California, Irvine; Electrodynamics Specialization, by Korea Advanced Institute of Science and Technology (KAIST). His major work is in electronics, software technologies, and related fields.

[This book is not affiliated with, authorized, sponsored, or approved by the institutions mentioned. The specific online courses cited above have not conferred University grades, course credits, or degrees, but certificates of completion.]

Perceptions About Reality Through Simulations by Software

A few illustrations and annotations about
The C++ Project

Marcos Tewfiq

Sao Paulo

Beelectronic

2021

Perceptions About Reality Through Simulations by Software
A few illustrations and annotations about The C++ Project

If you have any suggestions, please contact support@beelectronic.com.

Book cover: screen of a simulation using the software "The C++ Project (pro edition)", by Beelectronic™. Please visit us: www.beelectronic.com

ISBN-13: 978-65-991627-6-3   [Revised in June 2022.]

Dados Internacionais de Catalogação na Publicação (CIP)
(Câmara Brasileira do Livro, SP, Brasil)

```
Tewfiq, Marcos
   Perceptions about reality through simulations by
software : a few illustrations and annotations about
the C++ Project / Marcos Tewfiq. -- 1. ed. --
Piracicaba, SP : Beelectronic, 2021.

   ISBN 978-65-991627-6-3

   1. Projeto C + + Programação 2. Redes de
computadores - Métodos de simulação - Software
3. Simulação - Métodos 4. Simulação computacional
5. Software I. Título.


21-90821                              CDD-005.1068
```

Índices para catálogo sistemático:

1. Software : Desenvolvimento : Projetos : Métodos
      de simulação : Ciência da computação 005.1068

Maria Alice Ferreira - Bibliotecária - CRB-8/7964

To all the curious minds.

Contents

Introduction

In this book, we share perceptions about physics and the universe, which we had when working on the software described in "The C++ Project: A companion for learning the C++ programming language" [1].

We have worked on software to simulate a few elementary classical physics experiments. That software was written in the C++ programming language. Besides, we made into that book a simplified explanation of the algorithm and the programming language.

We have also worked on another version of that software, with a few modifications. This process has required testing that code on different computers, and the result is a better understanding of some algorithm problems. Nevertheless, an unexpected result appeared: we have increased our perception of physics and some other knowledge areas.

It is essential to register and share those perceptions. However, some may already be found by other researchers, and others may not have adequate scientific ground. However, the objective here is to demonstrate our reasoning and to share the experience of how our work on that software had resulted in those conclusions. We believe we could generalize this conclusion: working on simulations by software may change our understanding of the universe. Therefore, this book is also a work in philosophy, using computer science and physics as tools.

So, we are not going to compare the findings with the state of the art of science. The objective is not to misrepresent anyone but explain our experiences and reasons, in our own words, for a few critical conclusions, which extend through physics, computer science, economics, and other fields. About these other fields, which could be marketing as an example, we have no scientific background except the widespread knowledge. So, we are not presenting all the conclusions following the scientific procedures and validations, but they could be a starting point, another point in the cloud, or even disregarded.

The purpose is not to teach programming, but we will also share that code in Appendix A. That code is the same as what is in the mentioned book, with a few modifications concerning a simulation that now we call "info propagation".

If the reader wants to reproduce the results, the programming knowledge of the C++ language is necessary. It is essential to understand that code. Following our trajectory between the problems and findings will also be helpful.

So, we will likewise bring from that book a few lines about parallel programming and software race conditions. We think it will be valuable concerning the context of this book.

However, this book is not primarily about programming. The goal is just to share some findings. The reader without programming skills may ignore parallel programming and concurrency chapters.

We are going to illustrate with figures since the arts could reach the objective with equivalent precision. Therefore, this is not a mathematical approach but a kind of first intuitive approach, a hint of what could be the object of further studies.

Let us not forget that all of this has an important cultural element, what value someone gives to the knowledge of technologies, or its fundamental origins, which are the pure understanding of our universe through our tools, like physics and computer science.

We will use as the primary tools some simulations and the code behind them. The list of options is on its menu:

```
Please, choose one example or read parameters from file:

        [1] Three balls. (default)
        [2] One ball at rest. Piston with gravity.
        [3] Eight balls at rest. Piston with gravity.
        [4] Fifty balls (gas simulation approximation). Piston with gravity.
        [5] Planet and Satellite.
        [6] A Fictional Universe.
        [7] Five balls info propagation (intermediate period 20s).
        [8] Fifty balls info propagation (intermediate period 7s).
        [9] Fifty balls info propagation (1/2 speed).
        [10] Load parameters from file.


        Option:
```

We are going to use these simulations, which are based on the code of Appendix A and a slight variation of that code, pointing at what lines the alterations will be.

More than half of this book will be that code. We are not going to write much nor explain the ideas in detail. There is little content, but enough to register our discoveries and insights. So, our intended goal of this work is basically to register and share our few perceptions.

The simple things

Do people know what reality truly is, or do we think the reality is based on superficial perceptions?

During the software development of The C++ Project, we must make some simulations to test and validate the algorithm and its processing results. One of these simulations, the simplest of all, is about three balls that are in movement inside a cylinder.

The reader could now query Appendix A and see the Ball.cpp. We can see the complexity behind such a simple thing through the lines of the software.

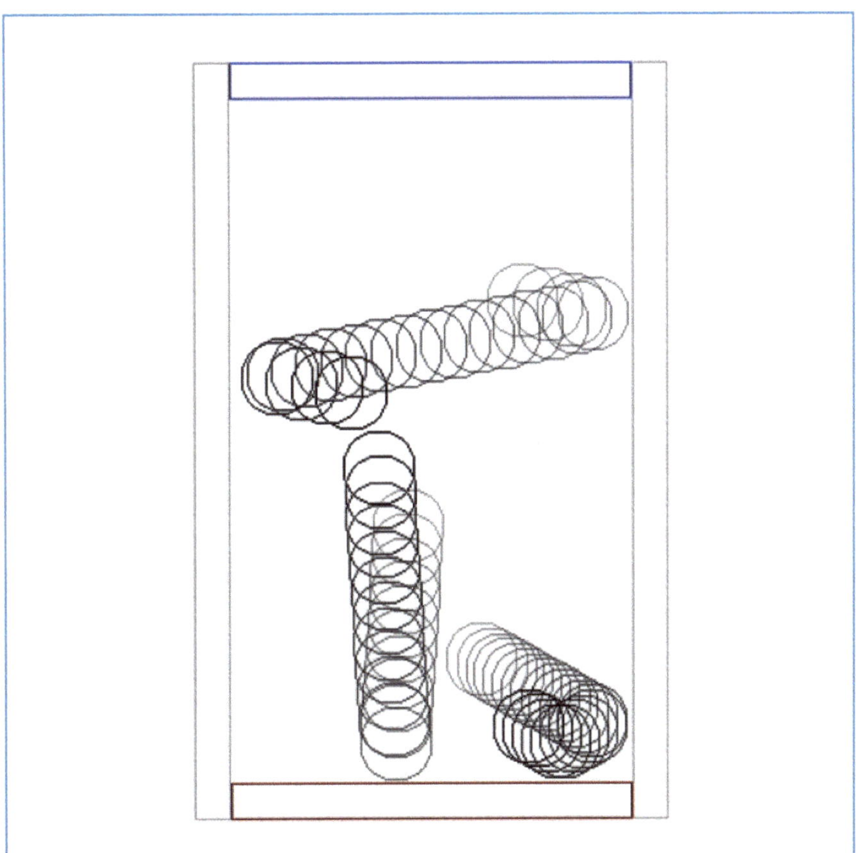

Figure 1 – Screen of simulation: "Three balls"; echo effect.

With just these three balls, as shown in figure 1, we could make a three-dimensional effect using some echo with decay (by another software). So, why could a third-dimensional figure emerge from a two-dimensional movement? In the software, we do not have a programmed z coordinate, so the echo effect is creating this third dimension. Maybe we could migrate one dimension just by adding some echo to our movements. Alternatively, maybe the reality is just echoing something that is moving on a two-dimensional plane.

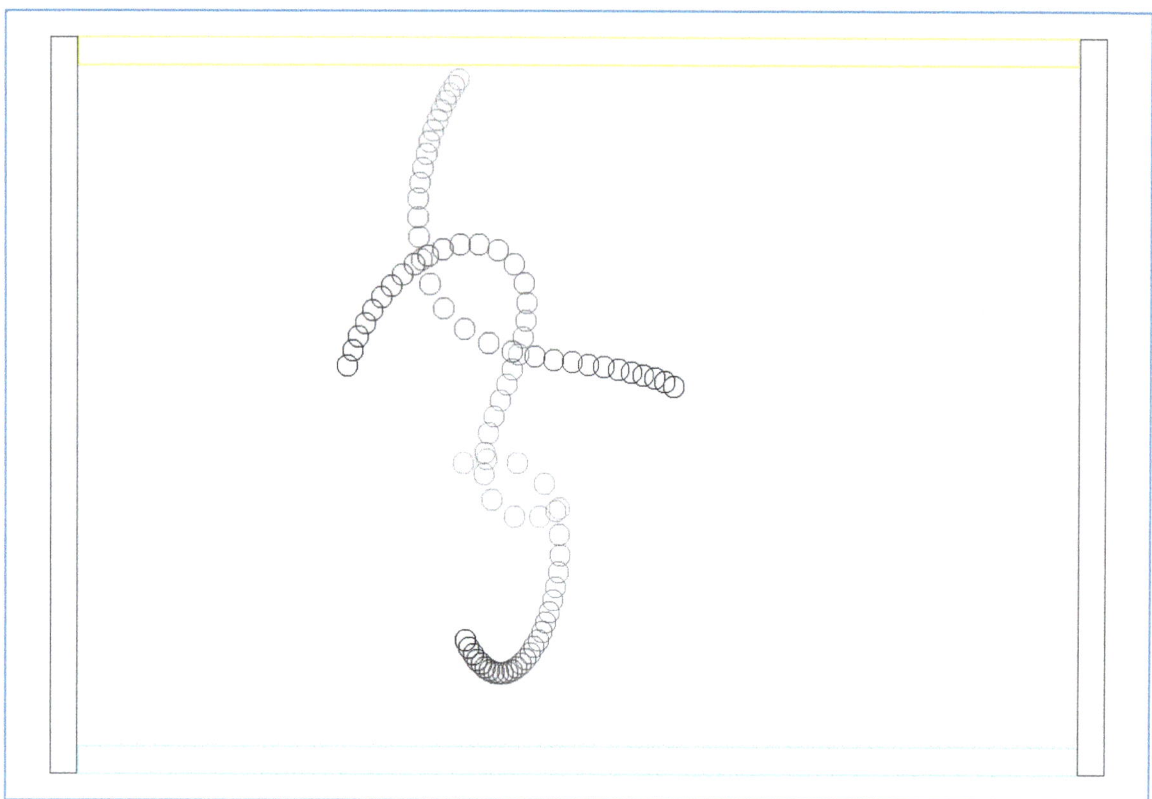

Figure 2 – Screen of simulation of three balls moving under mutual gravitation.

Another simple simulation is in figure 2. Again, we have just three balls moving under their gravitational forces. We have also added the echo effect.

Besides its simplicity, if we try to find the equations and the solution to find the positions at a given time, no complete analytic solution in closed form is possible (no exact calculation is possible), except for some exceptional cases [2] [3].

It means we can produce the figure above only through approximations, like this simulation. Therefore, we can see a very complex mathematical problem challenging physicists and mathematicians with such a simple thing.

The meaning of random phenomena

We have a simulation where eight balls are resting inside a cylinder without gravity. The top of the cylinder is a piston, which moves, and the piston is under gravity. The balls are in two groups, with four balls each. These four balls are perfectly aligned at the beginning of the simulation and form two queues, like the following first print screen:

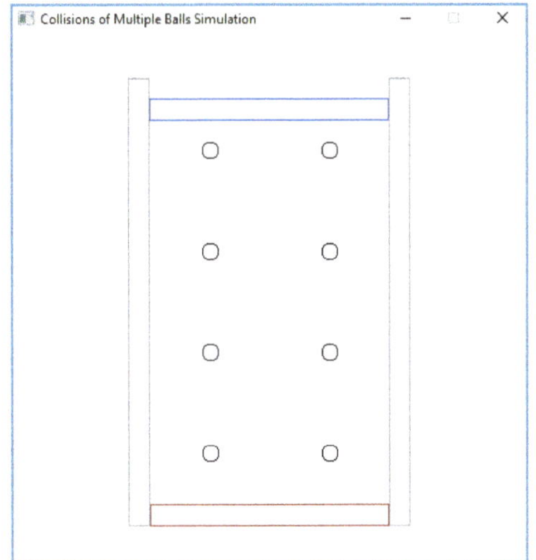

Figure 3 – Screen of simulation: "Eight balls at rest. Piston with gravity".

After the simulation starts, the piston will go down and collide with the balls, and each ball with another, propagating the movements. It is analogous to the transmission of "information":

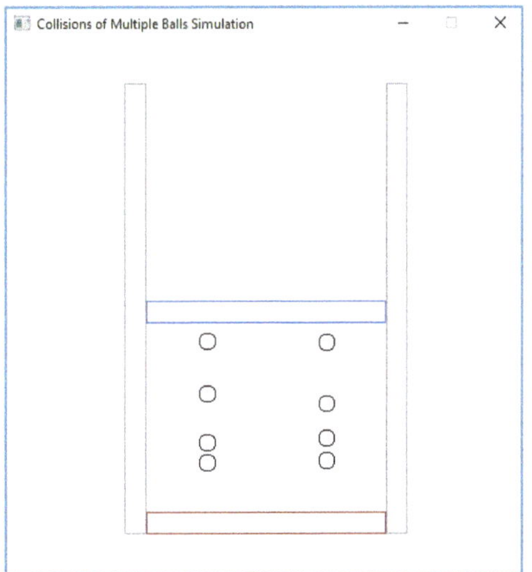

Figure 4 – Screen of simulation: "Eight balls at rest. Piston with gravity."

The process continues the same way, with the balls aligned and propagating the information (that they are aligned). However, sometimes, the process changes, and the alignment is lost. We think this is the result of a random process or something analogous to that:

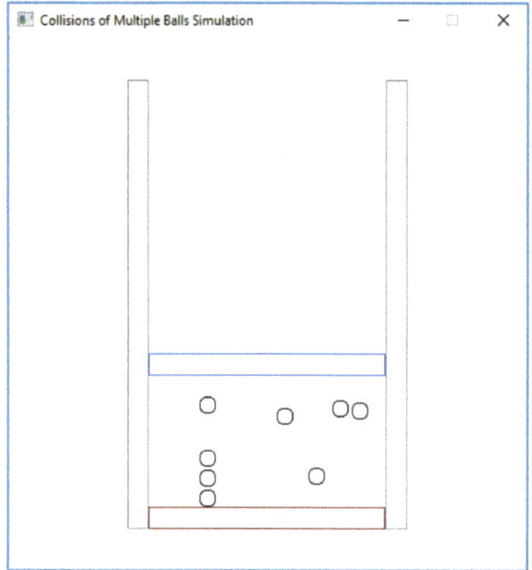

Figure 5 – Screen of simulation: "Eight balls at rest. Piston with gravity": loss of alignment in the queue on the right.

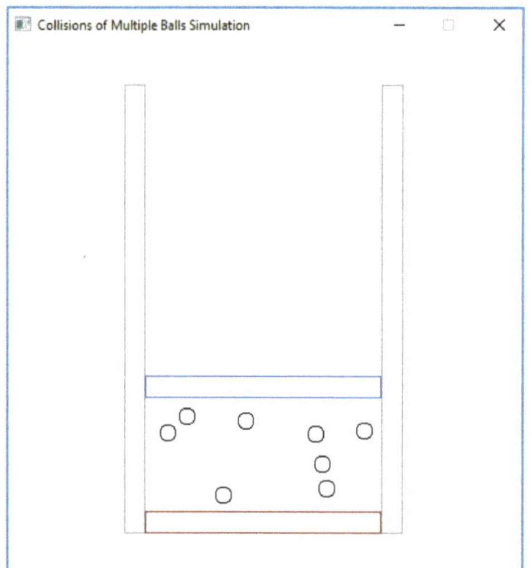

Figure 6 – Screen of simulation: "Eight balls at rest. Piston with gravity": prevalence of random movements.

Observing the simulation, we can reason about anything that is a chain of information being transmitted through time and movements, like the biological or chemical ones. It is clear that the random processes have a nature exactly the opposite of information, as they "destroy" information.

This simulation was useful to bring perception to a logical conclusion: it is very unlikely that something with nature exactly opposite of information could result in a bit of information. But it is even more unlikely that, at any moment, a bit of information could be randomly generated and could be able, despite its nature, to be continually transmitted by itself.

Order after randomness

The "Fifty balls (gas simulation approximation). Piston with gravity." starts with fifty balls distributed inside the cylinder. The balls do not have gravity, but the piston moves under gravity:

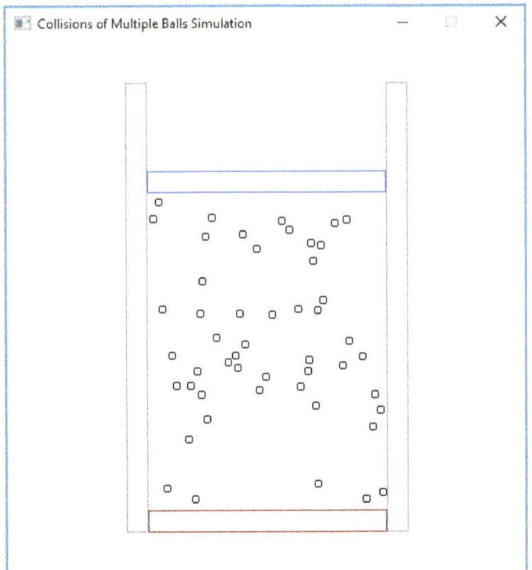

*Figure 7 – Screen of simulation: " Fifty balls (gas simulation approximation).
Piston with gravity.": the beginning of the simulation.*

The piston will go down and collide with the balls. In the process, the balls collide with themselves and will change their linear momentum, according to these equations:

$$m0*v0i + m1*v1i = m0*v0f + m1*v1f \quad \text{(Conservation of Linear Momentum)}$$

$$Ec0i + Ec1i = Ec0f + Ec1f \quad \text{(Conservation of Kinetic Energy)}$$

We choose to simulate collisions with the piston, like in a "gas", which we named as "gas" mode in the algorithm. The piston moves according to the force exerted on it by the balls. The program uses these equations for the piston:

$$F*(tf - ti) = m0*(v0i - v0f) \quad m0: \text{ball mass} \quad \text{(Linear Momentum-Impulse Theorem)}$$

$$F = m1*a \quad m1: \text{piston mass} \quad \text{(Newton's Second Law)}$$

```
Ball::simulate Ball _id=31  thread id=18080
Ball::simulate Ball _id=32  thread id=11184
Ball::simulate Ball _id=33  thread id=17240
Ball::simulate Ball _id=34  thread id=10512
Ball::simulate Ball _id=35  thread id=17992
Ball::simulate Ball _id=36  thread id=18220
Ball::simulate Ball _id=37  thread id=2276
Ball::simulate Ball _id=38  thread id=17020
Ball::simulate Ball _id=39  thread id=16272
Ball::simulate Ball _id=40  thread id=17856
Ball::simulate Ball _id=41  thread id=19192
Ball::simulate Ball _id=42  thread id=4596
Ball::simulate Ball _id=43  thread id=11664
Ball::simulate Ball _id=44  thread id=18120
Ball::simulate Ball _id=45  thread id=2160
Ball::simulate Ball _id=46  thread id=15680
Ball::simulate Ball _id=47  thread id=11424
Ball::simulate Ball _id=48  thread id=19176
Ball::simulate Ball _id=49  thread id=248
Ball::simulate Ball _id=50  thread id=18532
Ball::simulate Ball _id=51  thread id=10788
Ball::simulate Ball _id=52  thread id=7796
Ball::simulate Ball _id=53  thread id=16452
Ball::simulate Ball _id=54  thread id=16540
Time:0  balls:50  gas avg(1.0s) up force : 24.17    piston down force: 100.00    ~temp(bottom) : 0.00
Time:1  balls:50  gas avg(1.0s) up force : 29.79    piston down force: 100.00    ~temp(bottom) : 0.00
Time:2  balls:50  gas avg(1.0s) up force : 65.06    piston down force: 100.00    ~temp(bottom) : 0.00
Time:3  balls:50  gas avg(1.0s) up force : 66.06    piston down force: 100.00    ~temp(bottom) : 0.00
Time:4  balls:50  gas avg(1.0s) up force : 67.92    piston down force: 100.00    ~temp(bottom) : 0.00
```

Figure 8 – Screen of simulation: " Fifty balls (gas simulation approximation). Piston with gravity.": the beginning of simulation; printing of real-time data.

We can see in figure 8 some auxiliary real-time data printed by the software during the simulation. The first lines illustrate that each ball is running on a separate thread, like in a separate program. So, we have parallel processing.

The lines at the bottom of figure 8 show the up force that the balls are exerting on the piston. The downforce is exerted by gravity. When the up force is below the downforce, the acceleration points down, and the piston tends to point its velocity down and so tends to go down. This is what happens at the beginning of the simulation.

```
Time:0  balls:50  gas avg(1.0s) up force : 12.48    piston down force: 100.00    ~temp(bottom) : 0.00
Time:1  balls:50  gas avg(1.0s) up force : 31.80    piston down force: 100.00    ~temp(bottom) : 0.00
Time:2  balls:50  gas avg(1.0s) up force : 56.32    piston down force: 100.00    ~temp(bottom) : 0.00
Time:3  balls:50  gas avg(1.0s) up force : 52.98    piston down force: 100.00    ~temp(bottom) : 0.00
Time:4  balls:50  gas avg(1.0s) up force : 66.54    piston down force: 100.00    ~temp(bottom) : 0.00
Time:5  balls:50  gas avg(1.0s) up force : 44.08    piston down force: 100.00    ~temp(bottom) : 0.00
Time:6  balls:50  gas avg(1.0s) up force : 40.18    piston down force: 100.00    ~temp(bottom) : 0.00
Time:7  balls:50  gas avg(1.0s) up force : 45.59    piston down force: 100.00    ~temp(bottom) : 0.00
Time:8  balls:50  gas avg(1.0s) up force : 102.26   piston down force: 100.00    ~temp(bottom) : 0.00
Time:9  balls:50  gas avg(1.0s) up force : 165.34   piston down force: 100.00    ~temp(bottom) : 0.00
Time:10 balls:50  gas avg(1.0s) up force : 146.29   piston down force: 100.00    ~temp(bottom) : 0.00
Time:11 balls:50  gas avg(1.0s) up force : 227.01   piston down force: 100.00    ~temp(bottom) : 0.00
Time:12 balls:50  gas avg(1.0s) up force : 244.42   piston down force: 100.00    ~temp(bottom) : 0.00
Time:13 balls:50  gas avg(1.0s) up force : 259.93   piston down force: 100.00    ~temp(bottom) : 0.00
Time:14 balls:50  gas avg(1.0s) up force : 169.14   piston down force: 100.00    ~temp(bottom) : 0.00
Time:15 balls:50  gas avg(1.0s) up force : 110.23   piston down force: 100.00    ~temp(bottom) : 0.00
Time:16 balls:50  gas avg(1.0s) up force : 74.18    piston down force: 100.00    ~temp(bottom) : 0.00
Time:17 balls:50  gas avg(1.0s) up force : 62.00    piston down force: 100.00    ~temp(bottom) : 0.00
Time:18 balls:50  gas avg(1.0s) up force : 68.04    piston down force: 100.00    ~temp(bottom) : 0.00
Time:19 balls:50  gas avg(1.0s) up force : 58.93    piston down force: 100.00    ~temp(bottom) : 0.00
Time:20 balls:50  gas avg(1.0s) up force : 39.48    piston down force: 100.00    ~temp(bottom) : 0.00
Time:21 balls:50  gas avg(1.0s) up force : 51.37    piston down force: 100.00    ~temp(bottom) : 0.00
Time:22 balls:50  gas avg(1.0s) up force : 41.62    piston down force: 100.00    ~temp(bottom) : 0.00
Time:23 balls:50  gas avg(1.0s) up force : 29.54    piston down force: 100.00    ~temp(bottom) : 0.00
Time:24 balls:50  gas avg(1.0s) up force : 34.77    piston down force: 100.00    ~temp(bottom) : 0.00
Time:25 balls:50  gas avg(1.0s) up force : 57.35    piston down force: 100.00    ~temp(bottom) : 0.00
Time:26 balls:50  gas avg(1.0s) up force : 63.08    piston down force: 100.00    ~temp(bottom) : 0.00
```

Figure 9 – Screen of simulation: " Fifty balls (gas simulation approximation). Piston with gravity.": the beginning of simulation; printing of real-time data.

We can see that at the beginning of the simulation, the cyclic movement is visible (figure 9).

```
Time:664    balls:48    gas avg(1.0s) up force : 131.56    piston down force: 100.00    ~temp(bottom) : 0.00
Time:665    balls:48    gas avg(1.0s) up force : 100.58    piston down force: 100.00    ~temp(bottom) : 0.00
Time:666    balls:48    gas avg(1.0s) up force : 118.80    piston down force: 100.00    ~temp(bottom) : 0.00
Time:667    balls:48    gas avg(1.0s) up force : 85.71     piston down force: 100.00    ~temp(bottom) : 0.00
Time:668    balls:48    gas avg(1.0s) up force : 102.74    piston down force: 100.00    ~temp(bottom) : 0.00
Time:669    balls:48    gas avg(1.0s) up force : 80.54     piston down force: 100.00    ~temp(bottom) : 0.00
Time:670    balls:48    gas avg(1.0s) up force : 109.56    piston down force: 100.00    ~temp(bottom) : 0.00
Time:671    balls:48    gas avg(1.0s) up force : 66.97     piston down force: 100.00    ~temp(bottom) : 0.00
Time:672    balls:48    gas avg(1.0s) up force : 104.02    piston down force: 100.00    ~temp(bottom) : 0.00
Time:673    balls:48    gas avg(1.0s) up force : 89.00     piston down force: 100.00    ~temp(bottom) : 0.00
Time:674    balls:48    gas avg(1.0s) up force : 100.00    piston down force: 100.00    ~temp(bottom) : 0.00
Time:675    balls:48    gas avg(1.0s) up force : 113.68    piston down force: 100.00    ~temp(bottom) : 0.00
Time:676    balls:48    gas avg(1.0s) up force : 102.78    piston down force: 100.00    ~temp(bottom) : 0.00
Time:677    balls:48    gas avg(1.0s) up force : 117.38    piston down force: 100.00    ~temp(bottom) : 0.00
Time:678    balls:48    gas avg(1.0s) up force : 102.04    piston down force: 100.00    ~temp(bottom) : 0.00
Time:679    balls:48    gas avg(1.0s) up force : 110.43    piston down force: 100.00    ~temp(bottom) : 0.00
Time:680    balls:48    gas avg(1.0s) up force : 129.31    piston down force: 100.00    ~temp(bottom) : 0.00
Time:681    balls:48    gas avg(1.0s) up force : 78.81     piston down force: 100.00    ~temp(bottom) : 0.00
Time:682    balls:48    gas avg(1.0s) up force : 121.40    piston down force: 100.00    ~temp(bottom) : 0.00
Time:683    balls:48    gas avg(1.0s) up force : 94.21     piston down force: 100.00    ~temp(bottom) : 0.00
Time:684    balls:48    gas avg(1.0s) up force : 68.71     piston down force: 100.00    ~temp(bottom) : 0.00
Time:685    balls:48    gas avg(1.0s) up force : 101.79    piston down force: 100.00    ~temp(bottom) : 0.00
Time:686    balls:48    gas avg(1.0s) up force : 91.68     piston down force: 100.00    ~temp(bottom) : 0.00
Time:687    balls:48    gas avg(1.0s) up force : 90.64     piston down force: 100.00    ~temp(bottom) : 0.00
Time:688    balls:48    gas avg(1.0s) up force : 103.29    piston down force: 100.00    ~temp(bottom) : 0.00
Time:689    balls:48    gas avg(1.0s) up force : 94.23     piston down force: 100.00    ~temp(bottom) : 0.00
Time:690    balls:48    gas avg(1.0s) up force : 75.90     piston down force: 100.00    ~temp(bottom) : 0.00
Time:691    balls:48    gas avg(1.0s) up force : 130.42    piston down force: 100.00    ~temp(bottom) : 0.00
Time:692    balls:48    gas avg(1.0s) up force : 110.08    piston down force: 100.00    ~temp(bottom) : 0.00
```

Figure 10 – Screen of simulation: " Fifty balls (gas simulation approximation). Piston with gravity.": the cyclic movement is unclear; printing of real-time data.

But at a point in time, the randomness is great and prevails, as shown in figure 10.

```
Time:819    balls:48    gas avg(1.0s) up force : 94.62     piston down force: 100.00    ~temp(bottom) : 0.00
Time:820    balls:48    gas avg(1.0s) up force : 115.26    piston down force: 100.00    ~temp(bottom) : 0.00
Time:821    balls:48    gas avg(1.0s) up force : 77.44     piston down force: 100.00    ~temp(bottom) : 0.00
Time:822    balls:48    gas avg(1.0s) up force : 77.16     piston down force: 100.00    ~temp(bottom) : 0.00
Time:823    balls:48    gas avg(1.0s) up force : 93.15     piston down force: 100.00    ~temp(bottom) : 0.00
Time:824    balls:48    gas avg(1.0s) up force : 89.32     piston down force: 100.00    ~temp(bottom) : 0.00
Time:825    balls:48    gas avg(1.0s) up force : 93.58     piston down force: 100.00    ~temp(bottom) : 0.00
Time:826    balls:48    gas avg(1.0s) up force : 109.37    piston down force: 100.00    ~temp(bottom) : 0.00
Time:827    balls:48    gas avg(1.0s) up force : 122.77    piston down force: 100.00    ~temp(bottom) : 0.00
Time:828    balls:48    gas avg(1.0s) up force : 123.66    piston down force: 100.00    ~temp(bottom) : 0.00
Time:829    balls:48    gas avg(1.0s) up force : 120.75    piston down force: 100.00    ~temp(bottom) : 0.00
Time:830    balls:48    gas avg(1.0s) up force : 125.11    piston down force: 100.00    ~temp(bottom) : 0.00
Time:831    balls:48    gas avg(1.0s) up force : 91.01     piston down force: 100.00    ~temp(bottom) : 0.00
Time:832    balls:48    gas avg(1.0s) up force : 76.31     piston down force: 100.00    ~temp(bottom) : 0.00
Time:833    balls:48    gas avg(1.0s) up force : 91.83     piston down force: 100.00    ~temp(bottom) : 0.00
Time:834    balls:48    gas avg(1.0s) up force : 70.21     piston down force: 100.00    ~temp(bottom) : 0.00
Time:835    balls:48    gas avg(1.0s) up force : 73.50     piston down force: 100.00    ~temp(bottom) : 0.00
Time:836    balls:48    gas avg(1.0s) up force : 71.82     piston down force: 100.00    ~temp(bottom) : 0.00
Time:837    balls:48    gas avg(1.0s) up force : 58.98     piston down force: 100.00    ~temp(bottom) : 0.00
Time:838    balls:48    gas avg(1.0s) up force : 98.98     piston down force: 100.00    ~temp(bottom) : 0.00
Time:839    balls:48    gas avg(1.0s) up force : 130.94    piston down force: 100.00    ~temp(bottom) : 0.00
Time:840    balls:48    gas avg(1.0s) up force : 109.71    piston down force: 100.00    ~temp(bottom) : 0.00
Time:841    balls:48    gas avg(1.0s) up force : 127.48    piston down force: 100.00    ~temp(bottom) : 0.00
Time:842    balls:48    gas avg(1.0s) up force : 150.91    piston down force: 100.00    ~temp(bottom) : 0.00
Time:843    balls:48    gas avg(1.0s) up force : 112.84    piston down force: 100.00    ~temp(bottom) : 0.00
Time:844    balls:48    gas avg(1.0s) up force : 102.70    piston down force: 100.00    ~temp(bottom) : 0.00
Time:845    balls:48    gas avg(1.0s) up force : 91.20     piston down force: 100.00    ~temp(bottom) : 0.00
Time:846    balls:48    gas avg(1.0s) up force : 59.44     piston down force: 100.00    ~temp(bottom) : 0.00
Time:847    balls:48    gas avg(1.0s) up force : 68.46     piston down force: 100.00    ~temp(bottom) : 0.00
```

Figure 11 – Screen of simulation: " Fifty balls (gas simulation approximation). Piston with gravity.": the cyclic movement has returned; printing of real-time data.

Surprisingly, the cyclic movement returned, even after a period when the random nature was the major one.

When we saw the fluctuations, we thought about several situations where there is this kind of phenomenon, like the waves breaking on the beach. Maybe there is an analogy with several factors affecting the waves and the random movements of the balls. The result is a periodic movement that goes out and returns after some time.

Another analogy may exist with the market price fluctuations of a product around its "natural value". The natural value is equivalent to the contour conditions of the cylinder, like its size, the mass of the piston, and the mass of balls. So, it is expected some average value to the distance of the piston from the bottom of the cylinder. This is the "natural position". The fluctuations could be caused by two phenomena: the random collisions of the balls and the system trying to solve that randomness going toward what are its contour conditions.

Another perspective is that even with the random nature of the movement of the ball, the system is "programmed" to reach some well-defined movement. We have the order being generated with random data as the primary source of information.

Relating to the last chapter, these "contour conditions" possibly are what was missing in the unfolding of information.

Information is crucial to decision-making. However, what kind of information reaches us in this hyperconnected society?

In the "balls info propagation" simulations, our model has the premises: a) each source of information is represented by one ball; b) there are three stages: unaware, intermediate, and aware; c) when the ball receives the information, it goes to the intermediate stage, when stays a time, and then goes to the aware stage; d) during the intermediate stage, the ball transmits the information when collides with other that is in the unaware stage (aware ones are not able to transmit anymore).

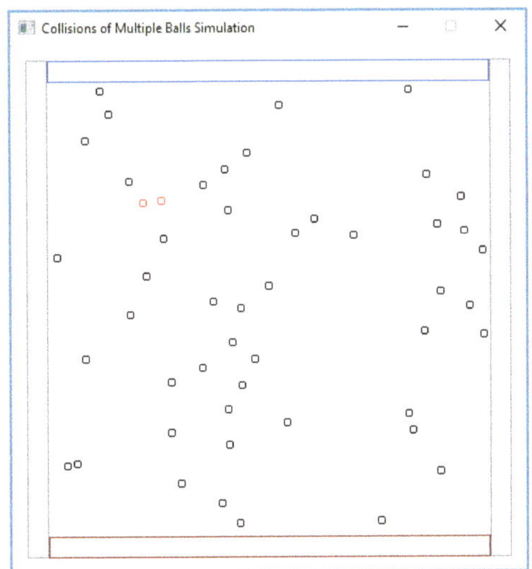

Figure 12 – Screen of simulation: Fifty balls info propagation (intermediate period 7s).": the beginning of the simulation.

At the beginning of the simulation, we can see in figure 12 that only a few balls have the new information (they are in red). We have used the "intermediate period" equal to 7s.

Each ball that is in red will collide with others and pass the new information. This will happen since the ball is red or is in the "intermediate stage". After that, the ball turns green, has the information but does not transmit anymore (lost interest in the propagation), or does not have that information in its memory (forgot the information).

It is reasonable to consider that the intermediate period is like a "memory" that lasts some time, and as important or memorable is the information as the duration in the memory.

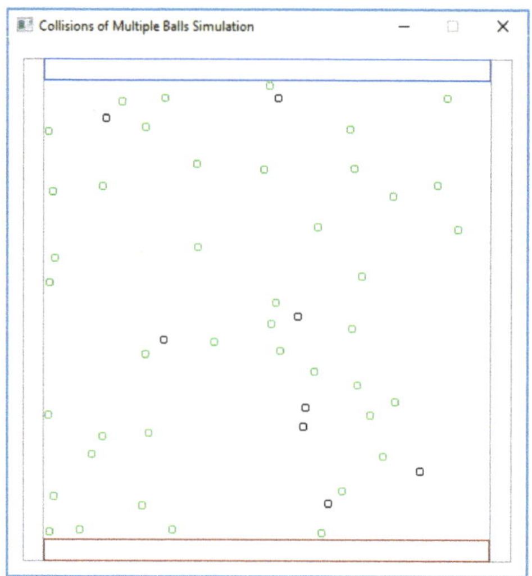

Figure 13 – Screen of simulation: Fifty balls info propagation (intermediate period 7s).": ending of simulation.

We can see, with the parameters used, that almost all the balls were informed (they are green), as only a few remain in the original color.

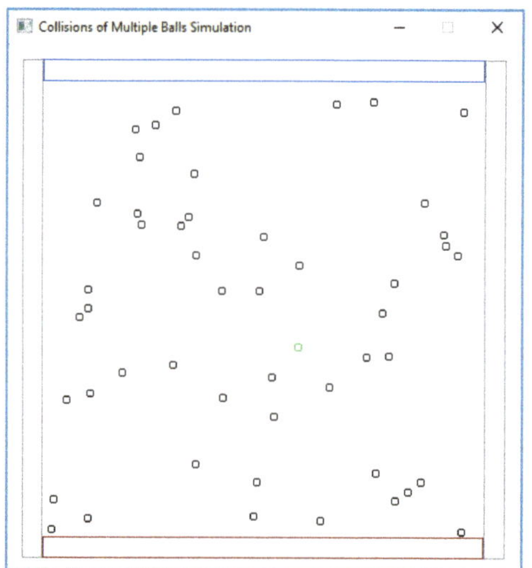

Figure 14 – Screen of simulation: Fifty balls info propagation (intermediate period 3s).": ending of simulation.

Using an intermediate period of 3s (half of anterior), representing information not so memorable (the ball "forgets" it in 3s), we have almost all balls unreached.

There are two significant parameters: a) the ball's speed (or energy); b) the intermediate time. This results in the "propagation speed". There is a critical point when the propagation speed surpasses the minimum required speed to reach a significant number of balls.

It is reasonable to consider, making a link with economic news, that the probability that the more unlikely facts, which by nature are more memorable, reach more people is greater than it would be. It seems that there is a bias toward incorrect decisions, as the information does not reflect the average values but shifts toward extreme ones.

Another conclusion is that the processes with greater intermediate periods have more chance to reach all the system as also the processes with greater energy (ball speeds). So, if we need to contain the propagation, this must be done as soon as possible because, after some time, the cost to do that is exponentially greater, and it is probable that we will not succeed unless we only want to slow down the process because this is always more probable than to contain it.

The processing power of the universe

In the "A Fictional Universe" simulation, we have 63 balls equally distributed and initially at rest inside a "square universe". They are under gravitational force. So, the balls attract each other, and initially, they all go to the center of this fictional universe.

We have made a series of pictures of this process, using an echo effect, with echo time -0.10s, number of echoes 15, and decay 0.95. It is possible to see the movements by observing the echoes of the ball's positions.

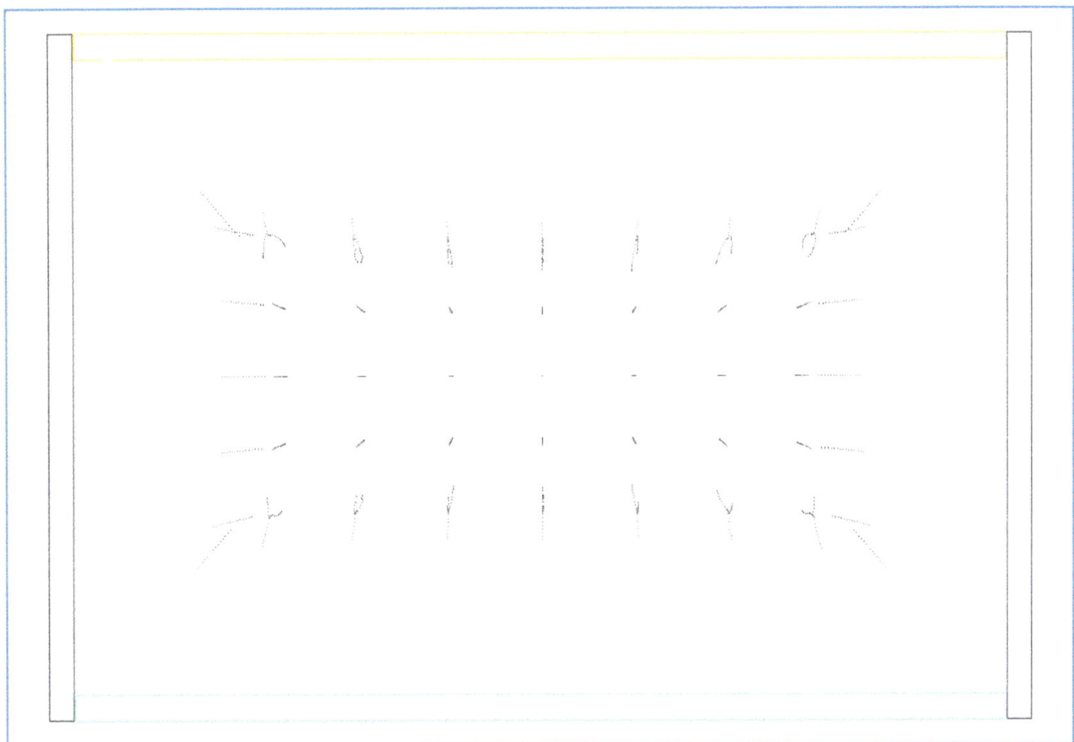

Figure 15 – Screen of simulation: "A Fictional Universe"; beginning of the simulation. Balls are going toward the center.

At figure 15, we see the balls going toward the center. The ball that is exactly at the center has stayed without movement. It is expected, as the sum of all forces actuating over it should be zero.

Below there is a sequence of figures to show the evolution of the simulation.

Figure 16 – Screen of simulation: "A Fictional Universe"; balls are going toward the center.

Figure 17 – Screen of simulation: "A Fictional Universe"; balls are forming clusters.

Figure 18 – Screen of "A Fictional Universe"; the beginning of the simulation. Balls are going toward the center.

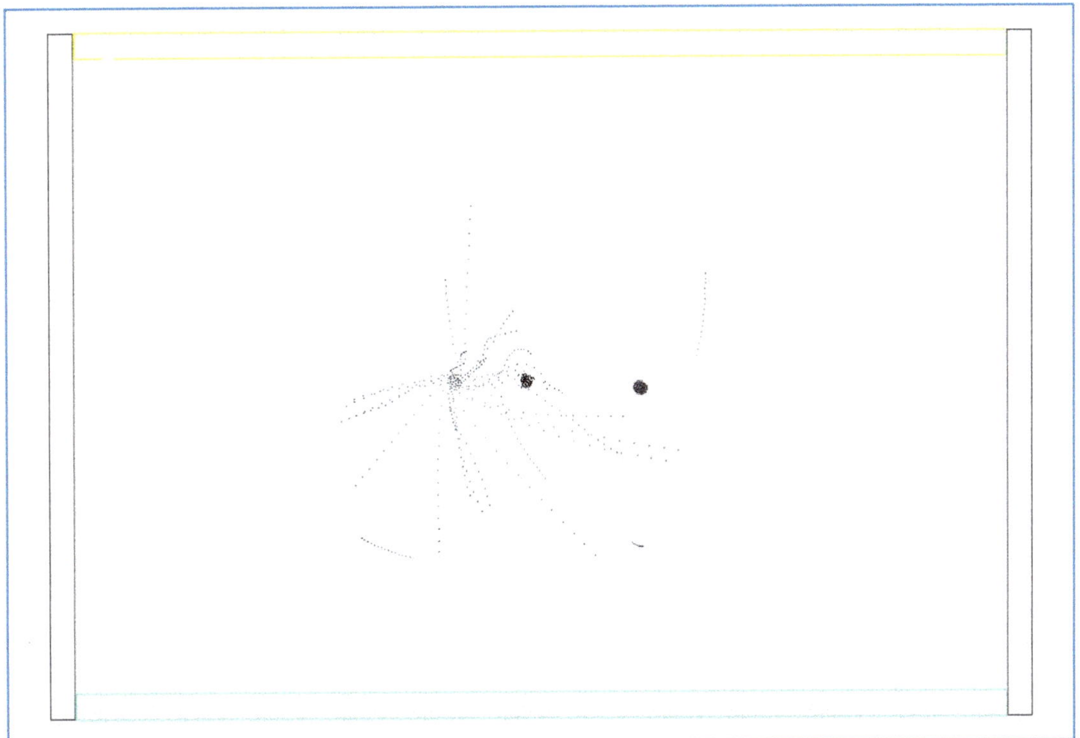

Figure 19 – Screen of simulation: "A Fictional Universe"; disintegration of the first cluster.

Figure 20 – Screen of simulation: "A Fictional Universe"; the third cluster is unstable.

Figure 21 – Screen of simulation: "A Fictional Universe"; stabilization of the third cluster.

Figure 22 – Screen of simulation: "A Fictional Universe"; disintegration of the second cluster.

Figure 23 – Screen of simulation: "A Fictional Universe"; instability of the third cluster.

At figure 17, we can see that the balls are trying to form clusters. At figure 18, three clusters are formed, with some balls trying to orbit them. We can see that there is one ball trying to orbit the first. At figure 19, the first cluster is disintegrating. This is caused by the algorithm (a negative force that we have added). In figure 20, we can see instability in the third cluster. According to figure 22, the third cluster becomes more stable. At figure 22, we can see that the third cluster disintegrated. Finally, in figure 23, although somewhat unstable, the third cluster remains, and we can see some balls trying to orbit it.

Now, we will repeat the experiment using a faster computer processor, which will give more processing power to the algorithm.

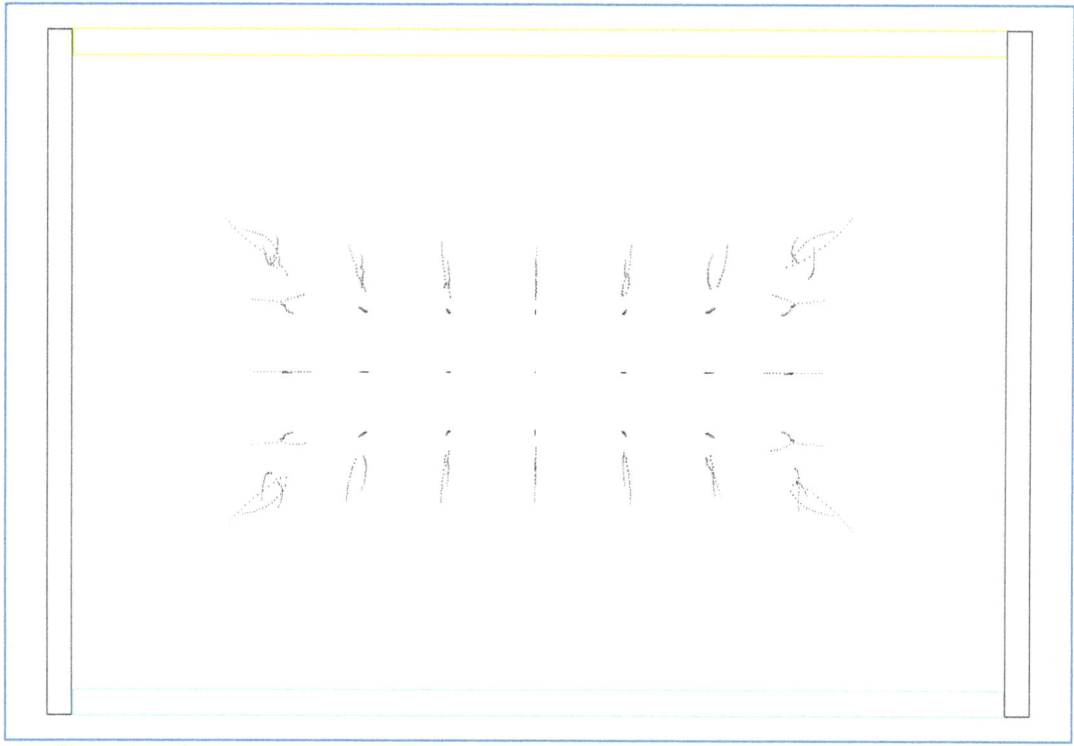

Figure 24 – Screen of simulation: "A Fictional Universe"; faster processor; the beginning of the simulation.

The simulation starts with the same result, the balls going toward the center.

Figure 25 – Screen of simulation: "A Fictional Universe"; balls are trying to form clusters.

Figure 26 – Screen of simulation: "A Fictional Universe"; two clusters; the second is stabilized.

Figure 27 – Screen of simulation: "A Fictional Universe"; two stable clusters.

Figure 28 – Screen of simulation: "A Fictional Universe"; the first cluster absorbs the second.

Figure 29 – Screen of simulation: "A Fictional Universe"; one big cluster has left.

Figure 30 – Screen of simulation: "A Fictional Universe"; one cluster, stable.

Figure 31 – Screen of simulation: "A Fictional Universe"; one cluster, stable.

Figure 32 – Screen of: "A Fictional Universe"; faster processor; echo effect with 200 echoes -0.1s; cluster as a "planet", and two balls trying to orbit it.

We can observe through the sequence above that, in a faster processor, the result is very different. It seems that our "negative force" (see lines 564-565, in "Ball.cpp") is not working because the cluster is not disintegrating.

We think this is because we have software race conditions. Software race conditions are situations when we have parallel processing, and the different threads try to change the same variable. So, the ball velocity changes as a result of the own ball processing, but this is canceled by another thread that is also changing that ball velocity.

Observing the code, we have a situation where the ball will change the other ball's velocity, as we see in line 587 (Ball.cpp). The important conclusion is not if this is true or not, but the emergence of the following concepts:

    a) race conditions can cause interferences;
    b) processing power can change the effect or occurrence of race conditions;
    c) altering the code can eliminate race conditions and change the results of the simulation.

In trying to get analog pieces, it is important to think about the double-slit experiment [4] [5] in quantum mechanics. In this experiment, a laser light source is pointed toward a plate with two parallel slits on it and a screen behind. The light passes the slits and forms a pattern on the screen that resembles waves, like as the light has passed simultaneously between the two slits like a wave, and these two wave sources generated by the two slits of the plate will interfere with each other and form the interference pattern on the screen.

The astonishing thing, however, is that it was verified that each photon of the light passes through one slit (in our case, we have just one ball passing through one slit). Nevertheless, if we put a detector to see in which slit the photon has passed, the interference pattern disappears, and instead, we have only the pattern formed as we have simple particles being thrown toward the slits.

We can think that there is a software processing our experiment, but as the particle is too small and too fast, the processor cannot solve the trajectory and give its best calculus based on the probability. It will consider that the particle (the ball) could pass through any of the slices (like a wave), and so we have the interference pattern. But if we change the experiment by putting a sensor to observe the particle, the software has changed, and the processor is now able to process accordingly, processing a particle as a particle would be.

The things become even more interesting when we remember another experiment, in special relativity, where we have two identical twins, but one travels on a journey into space at high-speed, so under acceleration to have that high speed [6]. When he returns, he is younger than his twin.

If we think that there is a kind of processing power limit to the universe, the solution of the simulation is that the universe tries to compensate for the acceleration (or maybe the velocity, if we think in terms of an absolute universal coordinate), slowing down the time, so it will succeed in processing the request.

We think, in principle, that these conclusions are supported by "The simulation hypothesis in physics" [7].

Concurrency

Typically, when the computer is executing our program, or when we think in the algorithm, we are reasoning in a sequence of events. When we call a function, we need to wait for its execution before we start executing the next instruction. This is the "**synchronous**" path of execution.

But we also can program the computer to execute the function while executing other things in parallel. In our example of the multi-ball collision simulator, we make the computer move the balls at the same time by functions that are running in parallel. This is called "**asynchronous**" execution: we do not have to wait. This is also called "**concurrency**" because we will have several codes wanting to run in the same CPU, concurring with its resources.

Some concepts to search are:

- "**parallel computing**", as a type of computation, and similarly "**concurrent computing**".
- "**synchronous**" and "**asynchronous**", referring to the path of execution.
- "**processes**" and "**threads**", relating to the resources (memory,
- "**address space**", processors, files, network connections) used by the program.
- "**concurrency**" support in C++, referring to the possibility of running multiple threads in parallel and the "**pthread**" library.
- **<thread>** header in C++.
- "**std::thread**", the thread class.
- "**thread object**", relating to the creation of a thread.
- "**main thread**", relating to the thread where "main" runs.
- "**join**" and "**detach**", referring to the thread object.
- "**thread constructor**", relating to its nature of "**variadic template**", a "**template**" that takes a variable number of arguments.
- "**std::move**" and "**std::ref**", relating to the way we pass the arguments to the thread function.

In C++, we make this by assigning a function to run into a "**thread**". This will make the function to be able to share the same memory, accessing the same variables of the main program or other functions running on other threads in the same program, also called "**process**". Typically, a program will run in one process, while it can have one thread for running its main function and other threads for functions or other tasks, if we ask to, normally in an asynchronous path in this case.

For working with threads in C++, we need to use the "Thread" class that is given by the "**thread**" library. We create an object of type **std::thread** and pass to it the function we want to execute in parallel. After that, while the function is running, we need to call the thread member function "**join**", which will only return when the thread run has been completed. In this way, we can be waiting for the thread to finish. If we do not do that, our main function will finish, the program will terminate, and our thread will still be running! This is not correct and may cause issues with the system.

Let us do something interesting: start a thread without calling "join". This is the code we are going to compile and run:

```cpp
1   #include <iostream>
2   #include <thread>
3
4   void threadFunction()
5   {
6       int i = 0;
7       for (int i = 0; i < 3; i++) {
8           std::this_thread::sleep_for(std::chrono::milliseconds(100)); // simulate work
9           std::cout << "Work in thread...\n";
10      }
11
12  }
13
14  int main()
15  {
16      // create thread
17      std::thread t(threadFunction);
18
19      // do something in main()
20      std::this_thread::sleep_for(std::chrono::milliseconds(50)); // simulate work
21      std::cout << "Finished work in main\n";
22
23      // wait for thread to finish
24      // t.join();
25
26      std::cout << "Finishing main\n";
27
28      return 0;
29
30  }
```

If we compile with g++, we need to include the support for the "pthread" library, with the flag "-pthread". For example, if the file above was named "Source.cpp", we need to command:

```
g++ Source.cpp -pthread
```

If we compile using an IDE, like Microsoft Visual Studio[1], it is not necessary.

In line 17, the program creates a thread and passes to it, as an argument, the function "threadFunction" that was declared in lines 4-12. The main code will print on the screen, even after the main thread has finished, causing an error (a debug error):

---

[1] This book is neither affiliated with, nor authorized, sponsored, or approved by, Microsoft Corporation.

```
Finished work in main
Finishing main
Work in thread...
Work in thread...
Work in thread...
(Error message)
```

Now, if we call the "join" by uncommenting line 24, the main function will wait:

```cpp
14    int main()
15    {
16        // create thread
17        std::thread t(threadFunction);
18
19        // do something in main()
20        std::this_thread::sleep_for(std::chrono::milliseconds(50)); // simulate work
21        std::cout << "Finished work in main\n";
22
23        // wait for thread to finish
24        t.join();
25
26        std::cout << "Finishing main\n";
27
28        return 0;
29
30    }
```

```
Finished work in main
Work in thread...
Work in thread...
Work in thread...
Finishing main
```

We can see that the "Finishing main" was printed after the work was finished in the thread. The "main" function has waited for the "threadFunction" running on the "t" thread to conclude its job.

In line 17 of the code above, we have called the thread constructor, passing to it, as an argument, the "threadFunction", a function that we have created before. In fact, if we want, we can pass more arguments, which will be interpreted by the constructor as the arguments to that function. Please, see the example:

```cpp
1    #include <iostream>
2    #include <thread>
3
4    void threadFunction(std::string threadName)
5    {
6        int i = 0;
```

```cpp
 7        for (int i = 0; i < 3; i++) {
 8            std::this_thread::sleep_for(std::chrono::milliseconds(100)); // simulate work
 9            std::cout << "Work in thread " << threadName << " ...\n";
10        }
11
12    }
13
14    int main()
15    {
16        // create thread
17        std::thread t(threadFunction, "Example");
18
19        // do something in main()
20        std::this_thread::sleep_for(std::chrono::milliseconds(50)); // simulate work
21        std::cout << "Finished work in main\n";
22
23        // wait for thread to finish
24        t.join();
25
26        std::cout << "Finishing main\n";
27
28        return 0;
29    }
```

```
Finished work in main
Work in thread Example ...
Work in thread Example ...
Work in thread Example ...
Finishing main
```

In line 4, the function was declared as having a parameter of type string. This will be printed on line 9. When we called the thread constructor, in line 17, we passed to it the name of the function and one string as arguments. Therefore, the thread constructor can receive a function and its arguments and will create a thread with those elements. This is possible because the constructor is defined with a "template", a "variadic" one, which can receive multiple arguments.

It is also possible to start threads with member functions. First, we create an object. Then, we call the tread constructor, passing to it the member function (the function that belongs to the class in which we have created the object), the object, and the arguments to be used by that member function. See the example in Appendix A, Ball.cpp, line 176 (no extra arguments are passed).

Concurrency 2

Now, our main goal is to pass the data between threads.

This is a complex topic. You do not need to search for everything on the first try. After that, please see the examples below and become more familiar with the subjects. We will not use all these concepts in the code example at the end of the book, but it is worth mentioning them. Some concepts to search are:

- **"concurrency bugs"**, relating to the errors we need to avoid in concurrent programming.
- "**data races**", relating to simultaneous reading and writing on shared data.
- "**critical sections**", the section of the code to be protected from data races.
- **<mutex>** header in C++.
- "**std::mutex**" means "mutual exclusion", the class used to signal critical sections of code that need exclusive access.
- "**lock**" and "**unlock**", relating to the "**mutex**".
- "**std::lock_guard**" class, relating to the "**mutex**".
- **<future>** header in C++.
- "**std::promise**" and "**std::future**" class, for one-way communication between threads.
- "**future::get**", relating to the blocking of the thread until it receives the value.
- **<condition_variable>** header in C++.
- "**std::condition_variable**" class, relating to the blocking of the thread until notified.

When we program our code to run in parallel, for example, in the simulation where we make each ball play in a separate thread (so the balls are all running in parallel), we will need some communication between the threads. It is done by "shared variables". For example, each ball needs to know the position of the others. The shared variable will be the coordinates of the ball, but this kind of communication can result in errors. For example, if we are reading an "x" coordinate of a ball with position (x, y) while it has changed its position and just write a new (x, y) in its coordinates. We have just read the "x", but before we read the "y", this data has changed. The result will be that we will have read the old "x" and the new "y" what is wrong!

The piece of code that contains the shared variables which we must protect from the simultaneous reads and writes is called the "critical section". When we have the "read" while the "write" is happening, it will be a "data race" problem. We can protect this section of the code by declaring an object of type "**mutex**" and calling the method "**lock**" at the beginning and "**unlock**" at the end of the section, so the other threads will not have access to it until the thread that is running finishes its job. The other threads will be waiting for the "unlock" of the section. Therefore, in an asynchronous path, this kind of use brings some synchronization.

There is a simpler way. We do not need to manage the "**mutex**" if we use the "**lock_guard**". This use prevents the problem that can happen if an exception (an error) occurs while executing code in the critical section. If this happens, because the variables are "locked", the code will probably freeze. Because the "lock_guard" will automatically unlock when we are out of scope, when the object is destructed, or when the exception occurs, the freeze will not happen.

See the example in Appendix A, in the file CylinderObject.cpp, lines 30-35. We are using the "lock_guard" at several places in the code. This means that we are protecting the shared variables from data races:

```cpp
void  CylinderObject::getPosition(double& x, double& y)
{
    std::lock_guard<std::mutex> lock(_mutex);
    x = _posX;
    y = _posY;
}
```

In the example above, we are reading the object position by calling the member function "getPosition", but only the thread that is running can access it, so it will access the "_posX" and "_posY" (which are the position of the cylinder) without interferences. These variables were protected from being changed while this thread was reading them. The other threads will wait (the object is "locked").

Observe that the "x" and "y" are passed by reference, so when we make "x = _posX", the "x" will load the value of "_posX," and this will reflect outside the member function, altering what the "x" and "y" at the caller is.

Nevertheless, there are situations where threads need to communicate specific data to other threads, which will be waiting for the data. This is where the "**promise**" and "**future**" classes are useful. In this case, we do not have a shared variable but a specific channel of communication for one-time use. Please, search for the concepts.

In our code example in Appendix A, Ball.cpp, lines 31-68, we are using another code structure, a "**message queue**" class, with the help of a "**condition_variable**" class and its member functions "**wait**" and "**notify_one**". It will work like a mailbox.

See the code:

```cpp
1   template <typename T>
2   class MessageQueue
3   {
4   public:
5       T receive();
6       void send(T&& msg);
7       int getSize();
8
9   private:
10      std::mutex _mutex;
11      std::condition_variable _cond;
12      std::deque<T> _queue;
13  };
14
15
16
```

```cpp
17   template <typename T>
18   T MessageQueue<T>::receive()
19   {
20
21       std::unique_lock<std::mutex> uLock(_mutex);
22       _cond.wait(uLock, [this] { return !_queue.empty(); });
23
24       T msg = std::move(_queue.back());
25       _queue.pop_back();
26
27       return msg;
28   }
29
30   template <typename T>
31   void MessageQueue<T>::send(T&& msg)
32   {
33       std::lock_guard<std::mutex> uLock(_mutex);
34       _queue.push_back(std::move(msg));
35       _cond.notify_one();
36   }
37
38   template <typename T>
39   int MessageQueue<T>::getSize()
40   {
41       std::lock_guard<std::mutex> uLock(_mutex);
42       return _queue.size();
43   }
```

In lines 1-13 above, we have the class declaration. This piece of code could be separated and saved in a header file (a file with extension .h). It is possible to observe what are the variables and what the class will do by the name of the functions.

We can see that the class uses a "**template**" mechanism that makes part of the class, the variables that will store the messages, independent of the data type. Therefore, it is possible to construct a queue for each data type with this same class.

In line 12, we have the queue declaration. On lines 10-11, we have the "**mutex**" and the "**condition_variable**" objects declaration, which will be used to manage the protection of the critical section, which in this case has the queue variable itself.

In lines 5-7, we have the functions prototypes. There are three functions: "receive", "send", and "getSize". The first is used to receive messages from the queue, the second to send, and the third to get the queue size. The functions definitions are on lines 17-43.

At the beginning of each function, on lines 21, 33, and 41, there is a class ("**unique_lock"** or "**lock_guard**") that will manage the "**mutex**". This shows that we will have a critical section following.

In line 22, we are using a "condition variable" object, named "_cond", calling its function "wait", which will make the thread wait until it receives a signal (see line 35) and the queue is not empty. The "wait' has two arguments. The first is the "uLock", the object that is managing the "mutex". The second is a lambda function, which will return true only if the queue is not empty (that will happen when we have data on it, or in other words after we have written data in the queue).

We could think that as we are in the critical section, the queue is locked to be written, so it will be impossible for another thread to update it. But the condition variable has the solution for this problem because it will temporally unlock the critical section until it receives a signal (from its function "notify_one"; see line 35) and will only unblock the thread (continues to execute the code after line 22) when the second argument of wait is true, or in this case, when the queue is not empty (when the queue is not empty, the lambda will return true).

Therefore, with the "send" function, lines 30-36, we write in the queue and send a signal to the condition variable in line 35. If we have a thread stopped in line 22, it will receive the signal, test if the queue is not empty, and as is the case, it will lock the critical section following, read the message from the queue (lines 24-25) and return the message (line 27).

When we need to have a class with a message queue to be able to send and receive messages from other threads, we just attach a message queue by declaring a member variable as a message queue object. For example, see line 115 at "Ball.h" in Appendix A. We have declared a "MessageQueue<CollisionData> _msgQueue" for communications between the "Ball" objects and the main function.

In line 140, in the main function, "Main.cpp" at Appendix A, we are starting a thread named "t1", passing to it as an argument a function "processPiston", and as one of the arguments to this function, the "balls" vector. In the "Piston.cpp", we have defined the "processPiston" function.

Inside that function, in line 116, we will get the message received from the ball after verifying if there is some message (line 113). We are calling the "receiveMsg" member function of the "ball". In the "Ball" class, line 157 of the file "Ball.cpp", we can see that the function is calling the "receive" method from the "_msgQueue" object. This is the "receive" method of our "message queue", as illustrated above, or in lines 31-47 of "Ball.cpp".

We are sending the messages in the "play" function of the "Ball" class on lines 383-384. This function will be running in another thread, as we can see in function "simulate", in line 176 of "Ball.cpp". This function "simulate" is called at the main function, "Main.cpp", line 155. So, it will start another thread.

Therefore, using this "message queue", the thread that is running the "ball", which is called in Ball::simulate, in line 176 of "Ball.cpp" ("Main.cpp", main(), line 155), will send the messages to the thread that is running the "processPiston" function, which is called in line 140 of the main function ("Main.cpp", main(), line 140).

Practice

Let us do an exercise with a situation that will occur in our Multi-ball Collision Simulator, with two threads reading and writing on each other. The goal is to see if when one class locks its variables, the other cannot access it. Another is to see if when one class locks the variables of the other class, the other must wait until the unlock.

The code will have two objects that, each play, will change itself and the other. See below:

```cpp
#include <string>
#include <mutex>
#include <vector>
#include <iostream>

std::mutex mtxCout;

class Board: public std::enable_shared_from_this<Board>
{
public:
    Board() {
        _message = "";
        _id = _idCnt;
        _idCnt++;
        _waitTime = 0;
    };
    void setMessage(std::string message) {
        _message = message;
        printBoard();
    }
    void setWaitTime(int waitTime) { _waitTime = waitTime; }
    void setBoards(std::vector<std::shared_ptr<Board>> boards) {
        _boards = boards;
    }
    int getId() { return _id; }

    void play() {
        mtxCout.lock();
        std::cout << "board(" << _id << ") begin of play() with " <<
            "thread id=" << std::this_thread::get_id() << std::endl;
        mtxCout.unlock();

        // begin of critical section
        board_mutex.lock();
        // write on this board
        setMessage("board(" + std::to_string(_id) + ") mutex locked");
        std::this_thread::sleep_for(
            std::chrono::milliseconds(_waitTime));

```

```cpp
        for (auto board : _boards) {
            // write on another board
            if (board->getId() != getId()) {
                board->setMessage("board(" + std::to_string(_id) +
                    ") writing on the board(" +
                    std::to_string(board->getId()) + ")");
                std::this_thread::sleep_for(std::chrono::milliseconds(_waitTime));
            }
        }

        setMessage("board(" + std::to_string(_id) + ") unlocked");
        // end of critical section
        board_mutex.unlock();

        mtxCout.lock();
        std::cout << "board(" << getId() << ") end of play()" << std::endl;
        mtxCout.unlock();
    }

    void printBoard() {
        mtxCout.lock();
        std::cout << _message << std::endl;
        mtxCout.unlock();
    }

    std::mutex board_mutex;

private:
    static int _idCnt;
    int _id, _waitTime;
    std::string _message;
    std::vector<std::shared_ptr<Board>> _boards;
};

int Board::_idCnt = 0;

int main() {
    std::vector<std::shared_ptr<Board>> boards;
    for (int nb = 0; nb < 2; nb++) {
        boards.push_back(std::make_shared<Board>());
    }
    boards.at(0)->setBoards(boards);
    boards.at(0)->setWaitTime(3000);
    boards.at(1)->setBoards(boards);
    boards.at(1)->setWaitTime(1000);
    std::thread t0(&Board::play, boards.at(0));
    std::thread t1(&Board::play, boards.at(1));
    t0.join();
    t1.join();
}
```

The core of the class is the function "play", in lines 27-57. This function will print when it has started, showing the thread "id". After that, it will try to change the data of the other "board" (that is running on another thread). It will do that with the function "setMessage".

The "board" 1 has a shorter cycle (line 84), 1000ms compared to 3000ms of "board" 0. The purpose is to see if it can change the data inside "board" 0, when the "mutex" in that class (in "board" 0) be locked. Let us see the printed results:

```
board(0) begin of play() with thread id=15840
board(1) begin of play() with thread id=9028
board(0) mutex locked
board(1) mutex locked
board(1) writing on the board(0)
board(1) unlocked
board(1) end of play()
board(0) writing on the board(1)
board(0) unlocked
board(0) end of play()
```

As seen above, the "board" 1 succeed in changing the data inside "board" 0. This is because when the "board" 1 is writing in the "_message" of board 0, through the "setMessage", it is not locking the same "mutex" (the "mutex" of "board" 0), but only its own "mutex".

Therefore, the solution is to make a "lock" on the "mutex" of the other class, before calling the "setMessage". See the code:

```cpp
for (auto board : _boards) {
    // write on another board
    if (board->getId() != getId()) {
        board->board_mutex.lock();
        board->setMessage("board(" + std::to_string(_id) +
            ") writing on the board(" +
            std::to_string(board->getId()) + ")");
        std::this_thread::sleep_for(std::chrono::milliseconds(_waitTime));
        board->board_mutex.unlock();
    }
}
```

We just created two statements inside the for-loop. One at the beginning, the other at the end, with the lock/unlock commands. Nevertheless, the result was:

```
board(1) begin of play() with thread id=13496
board(1) mutex locked
board(0) begin of play() with thread id=13984
board(0) mutex locked
```

The code will halt here and show an error message. The reason is that as one thread is already locked, it is not possible to lock it again. When the "board" 1 tries to lock the mutex of "board" 0, it has already been locked by the "board" 0, so it is not possible to lock it again. It must be unlocked. However, the "board" 0 will only unlock after the for-loop and succeed in locking the "board" 1. Therefore, both threads will be waiting for the other to complete, but it will not be possible because it depends on a lock of something already locked. This is a scenario called a "deadlock".

Instead of having a mutex for each object, we can make the mutex "static", so all the objects will share the same (it will belong to the class):

```cpp
static std::mutex board_mutex;
```

The other adjustment is the necessity of declaring the static variable in the global context, just before the "main" function:

```cpp
int Board::_idCnt = 0;
std::mutex Board::board_mutex;

int main() {
```

Now the results will be:

```
board(0) begin of play() with thread id=936
board(1) begin of play() with thread id=7372
board(0) mutex locked
board(0) writing on the board(1)
board(0) unlocked
board(0) end of play()
board(1) mutex locked
board(1) writing on the board(0)
board(1) unlocked
board(1) end of play()
```

The goal was achieved. We can see that the "board(0)" starts locking the mutex. After that, it will complete its work without the interference of "board(1)". Nevertheless, if we have multiple boards, with each one locking the same mutex, we will have lost the benefits of parallelism since the threads will be running like a synchronous path.

Another important practice is to find the race conditions in the code of Appendix A, a much more complex exercise. That code has a few critical issues, but we are not able to say that it has errors. This is because it will depend upon the context and objectives.

If we are looking for a perfect code in terms of computer science, that code may have a few errors regarding race conditions and other issues. However, we have an intuition that if the goal is to represent the physics of the universe, we must not discard the possibility that the race conditions and their unpredictable consequences could better represent what would be the correct results.

References

[1] M. Tewfiq, The C++ Project: A companion for learning the C++ programming language, 2 ed., Piracicaba, SP, Brazil: Beelectronic, 2021.

[2] Britannica, The Editors of Encyclopaedia, "three-body problem", Encyclopedia Britannica, 3 March 2021. [Online]. Available: https://www.britannica.com/science/three-body-problem. [Accessed 17 November 2021].

[3] S. J. Peale, "celestial mechanics", Encyclopedia Britannica, 3 February 2015. [Online]. Available: https://www.britannica.com/science/celestial-mechanics-physics. [Accessed 17 November 2021].

[4] Wikipedia contributors, "Double-slit experiment", Wikipedia, The Free Encyclopedia, 13 November 2021. [Online]. Available: https://en.wikipedia.org/w/index.php?title=Double-slit_experiment&oldid=1054974272. [Accessed 16 November 2021].

[5] PBS Space Time, "The Quantum Experiment that Broke Reality", PBS Digital Studios, 27 July 2016. [Online]. Available: https://youtu.be/p-MNSLsjjdo. [Accessed 15 November 2021].

[6] Wikipedia contributors, "Twin paradox", Wikipedia, The Free Encyclopedia, 14 September 2021. [Online]. Available: https://en.wikipedia.org/w/index.php?title=Twin_paradox&oldid=1044251756. [Accessed 16 November 2021].

[7] Wikipedia contributors, "Simulation hypothesis", Wikipedia, The Free Encyclopedia, 15 November 2021. [Online]. Available: https://en.wikipedia.org/w/index.php?title=Simulation_hypothesis&oldid=1055436345. [Accessed 16 November 2021].

Appendix A

Globals.h

```cpp
#ifndef GLOBALS_H
#define GLOBALS_H

// Simulation mode
double gas_mode = 0;                    // choose the mode of simulation
                                        // "standard"(0) or "gas"(1)
// Ball
int nballs = 8;                         // 100 max approx
double ball_radius = 8;                 // max 0.5 * WALL_WIDTH approx
double ball_speed = 0;                  // pixels/s (SPPED < RADIUS * 200 max approx)
double ball_mass = 0.2;                 // 0.01 * piston_mass min approx
double ball_gravity = 0;                // if zero, simulate gas
double ball_G = 0;                      // gravitational constant
const double G_mult = 1e5;
int push_pull = 1;                      // push-pull balls apart after collision
double coef_rest = 1.0;                 // coef. restitution collision between balls

int is_testing = 0;                     // choose the testing mode (1) or normal mode (0)
double ball0_speed = 10;                // in testing mode, set the first two balls
double ball0_vel_angle = 0;
double ball0_x = -1;
double ball0_y = -1;
double ball0_radius = -1;
double ball0_mass = -1;

double ball0_time = 0;                  // will update the velocity after time
double ball0_delta_speed = 0;
double ball0_delta_angle = 0;

double ball1_speed = 10;
double ball1_vel_angle = -180;
double ball1_x = -1;
double ball1_y = -1;
double ball1_radius = -1;
double ball1_mass = -1;

// DONE: create a global control variable for "info" simulation option
int is_info_simulation = 0;             // normal mode (0) or "info" simulation (1)

// DONE: create a variable that represents the intermediate stage
double inter_period = 7.0; // time in sec

// Piston
double piston_mass = 10.0;
double piston_gravity = 10.0;   // if zero, piston stops
```

```cpp
47    // Bottom
48    double bottom_temp_min = 0.0;
49    double bottom_temp_max = 100.0;
50
51    // Background color (black:0 white:1)
52    int background_color = 1;
53
54    // Screen and wall width dimensions
55    double screen_width = 480;
56    double screen_height = 480;
57    double wall_width = 20;
58
59    // cylinder position and dimensions
60    double cylinder_center_position_x = screen_width / 2;
61    double cylinder_center_position_y = screen_height / 2;
62
63    double percent_width = 0.50;
64    double cylinder_width = screen_width * percent_width;
65
66    double percent_height = 0.80;
67    double cylinder_height = screen_height * percent_height;
68
69    double zoom_factor = 1.0;
70
71    #endif
```

```cpp
1    #ifndef CylinderObject_H
2    #define CylinderObject_H
3
4    #include <vector>
5    #include <thread>
6    #include <mutex>
7
8
9    enum class ObjectType
10   {
11       noObject,
12       objectBall,
13       objectWall,
14   };
15
16   class CylinderObject
17   {
18   public:
19       // constructor / destructor
20       CylinderObject();
21       ~CylinderObject();
22
23       // getters / setters
24       int getID() { return _id; };
25       // position of object on canvas (Ball, Wall, or Piston)
26       void setPosition(double x, double y);
27       void getPosition(double& x, double& y);
28       // velocity of object
29       void setVelocity(double velX, double velY);
30       void getVelocity(double& velX, double& velY);
31       // speed of object
32       double getSpeed();
33       // mass of object
34       void setMass(double m);
35       double getMass();
36       ObjectType getType() { return _type; }
37
38       static std::mutex mtxCout;          // mutex shared by all cylinder objects for
39       // protecting cout
40
41       // typical behaviour methods
42       virtual void simulate() {};         // This will be implemented by the Ball class
43
44   protected:
45       // member attributes
46       ObjectType      _type;              // identifies the class type
47       int _id;                            // every cylinder object has its own id
48       double      _posX, _posY;           // object position in pixels (center)
49       double _velX, _velY, _speed;        // velocity and speed in pixels/s
50       double _mass;                       // object mass
51
```

```cpp
52      std::vector<std::thread> _threads;      // holds all threads that have been launched
53                                              // within this object
54      std::mutex     _mutex;                  // mutex to protect member attributes
55
56  private:
57      // member attributes
58      static int _idCnt;                      // global variable for counting ids
59
60  };
61
62
63  #endif
```

```cpp
1   #ifndef BALL_H
2   #define BALL_H
3
4   #include <mutex>
5   #include <deque>
6   #include <condition_variable>
7   #include <ctime>
8
9   #include "CylinderObject.h"
10  #include "Wall.h"
11
12
13  // forward declarations to avoid including cycle
14  class Wall;
15
16  // This is a message queue class for sending messages between threads
17  template <typename T>
18  class MessageQueue
19  {
20  public:
21      T receive();
22      void send(T&& msg);
23      int getSize();
24
25  private:
26      std::mutex _mutex;
27      std::condition_variable _cond;
28      std::deque<T> _queue;
29  };
30
31  enum class CollisionType {
32      wallCollision,
33      bottomCollision,
34      pistonCollision,
35  };
36
37  struct CollisionData {
38      CollisionType type;
39      double velY;
40  };
41
42  class Ball : public CylinderObject, public std::enable_shared_from_this<Ball>
43  {
44  public:
45      // constructor / destructor
46      Ball();
47
48      // getters / setters
49      void setWalls(std::vector<std::shared_ptr<Wall>> walls) { _walls = walls; }
50      void setBalls(std::vector<std::shared_ptr<Ball>> balls) { _balls = balls; }
51
```

```cpp
52      void setRadius(double r) { _radius = r; }
53      double getRadius() { return _radius; }
54
55      // This method will set a direction, calculating Vx and Vy based on speed and angle
56      void setSpecificDirection(double speed, double angle);
57
58      // This method will choose a random direction for the ball
59      void setRandomDirection(double speed);
60
61      // Gravitational Acceleration
62      void setGravity(double ball_gravity) { _ball_gravity = ball_gravity;  }
63      double getGravity() { return _ball_gravity; }
64
65      // Gravitational Constant (multiplied by a factor G_mult)
66      void setG(double ball_G) { _coef_G = ball_G; }
67      double getG() { return _coef_G; }
68
69      // Flag to set the "gas" mode model (piston counts the collisions)
70      void setGasMode(bool gas_mode) { _gas_mode = gas_mode;  }
71
72      // Coefficient of Restitution (for inelastic collisions)
73      void setCoefRestitution(double coef_e) { _coef_e = coef_e; }
74      double getCoefRestitution() { return _coef_e; }
75
76      // DONE: Get "info" simulation data (this operations need to be protected with mutex)
77      void setInfoStage(int stage);
78      int getInfoStage();
79      void setPropagationTime(std::time_t time);
80      std::time_t getPropagationTime();
81
82      // typical behaviour methods
83      bool dataIsAvailable();        // inform that there is a message from other thread
84      CollisionData receiveMsg();    // receive msg from other thread (msg stored in queue)
85      void simulate();            // process ball movements
86      void setShutdown();          // set the flag to exit while-loop in simulate()
87
88      // miscellaneous
89      std::shared_ptr<Ball> get_shared_this() { return shared_from_this(); }
90      std::mutex ball_mutex;
91
92  private:
93      // typical behaviour methods
94      void play();
95      // check if has collided with a wall
96      bool checkWallCollision(double nextX, double nextY, std::shared_ptr<Wall> wall);
97      // check if has collided with another ball
98      bool checkBallCollision(double nextX, double nextY, std::shared_ptr<Ball> ball);
99      // receive direct message to shutdown (exit while-loop)
100     bool getShutdown();
101
102     // member attributes
103     double _radius;                // ball radius
104     double _ball_gravity;          // gravity
105     double _coef_G;                // gravitational constant
106     bool _gas_mode;                // simulation mode
```

```cpp
107      double _coef_e;                          // restitution coefficient
108
109      // DONE: attributes to control "info" stage, time from last collision
110      int _info_stage;    // "info" stage: 0:"unaware"; 1:"intermediarie"; 2:"aware"
111      std::time_t _propagation_time;        // time at propagation
112
113      std::vector<std::shared_ptr<Wall>> _walls;  // walls of cylinder on which ball is on
114      std::vector<std::shared_ptr<Ball>> _balls;  // balls of cylinder on which ball is on
115      MessageQueue<CollisionData> _msgQueue;     // msg queue for communications with main
116      bool _shutDown;                        // ask ball to end simulation
117 };
118
119 #endif
```

```cpp
#ifndef WALL_H
#define WALL_H

#include "CylinderObject.h"

enum class WallType
{
    lateral,
    piston,
    cover,
    bottom,
};

class Wall : public CylinderObject, public std::enable_shared_from_this<Wall>
{
public:
    // constructor / destructor
    Wall();

    // getters / setters
    // size (width and height)
    void setSize(double w, double h);
    void getSize(double& w, double& h);

    // heat or temperature
    void setHeat(double ht);
    double getHeat();

    // type of the wall: lateral, piston, bottom
    void setWallType(WallType type) { _wallType = type; }
    WallType getWallType() { return _wallType; }

    // miscellaneous
    std::shared_ptr<Wall> get_shared_this() { return shared_from_this(); }

    std::mutex wall_mutex;        // wall mutex

private:

    // member attributes
    double _width, _height;       // object width and height in pixels
    double _temp;                 // wall temperature
    WallType _wallType;           // wall type

};


#endif
```

```cpp
#ifndef PISTON_H
#define PISTON_H

#include "Ball.h"
#include "Wall.h"

// Prototype of the "processPiston", which will process the piston dynamics
void processPiston(std::shared_ptr<Wall> piston, std::shared_ptr<Wall> bottom,
    std::vector<std::shared_ptr<Ball>> balls, bool& finish);

#endif
```

```cpp
1    #include <algorithm>
2
3    #include "CylinderObject.h"
4
5
6    // init static variables
7    int CylinderObject::_idCnt = 0;
8    std::mutex CylinderObject::mtxCout;
9
10   CylinderObject::CylinderObject()
11   {
12       _type = ObjectType::noObject;
13       _id = _idCnt;
14       _posX = 0;
15       _posY = 0;
16       _velX = 0;
17       _velY = 0;
18       _speed = 0;
19       _mass = 0;
20       _idCnt++;
21   }
22
23   void CylinderObject::setPosition(double x, double y)
24   {
25       std::lock_guard<std::mutex> lock(_mutex);
26       _posX = x;
27       _posY = y;
28   }
29
30   void  CylinderObject::getPosition(double& x, double& y)
31   {
32       std::lock_guard<std::mutex> lock(_mutex);
33       x = _posX;
34       y = _posY;
35   }
36
37   void CylinderObject::setVelocity(double velX, double velY)
38   {
39       std::lock_guard<std::mutex> lock(_mutex);
40       _velX = velX;
41       _velY = velY;
42       _speed = sqrt(pow(velX, 2) + pow(velY, 2));
43   }
44
45   void CylinderObject::getVelocity(double& velX, double& velY)
46   {
47       std::lock_guard<std::mutex> lock(_mutex);
48       velX = _velX;
49       velY = _velY;
50   }
51
```

```cpp
52   double CylinderObject::getSpeed()
53   {
54       std::lock_guard<std::mutex> lock(_mutex);
55       _speed = sqrt(pow(_velX, 2) + pow(_velY, 2));
56       return _speed;
57   }
58
59   void CylinderObject::setMass(double mass)
60   {
61       _mass = mass;
62   }
63
64   double CylinderObject::getMass()
65   {
66       return _mass;
67   }
68
69   CylinderObject::~CylinderObject()
70   {
71       // set up thread barrier before this object is destroyed
72       std::for_each(_threads.begin(), _threads.end(), [](std::thread& t) {
73           t.join();
74       });
75   }
```

```cpp
1    #include <iostream>
2    #include <thread>
3    #include <future>
4    #include <memory>
5    #include <random>
6    #include <algorithm>
7    #include <cmath>
8    #include <array>
9    #include <iomanip>
10   #include <string>
11   #include <ctime>
12
13   #include "Ball.h"
14
15   // Variables defined at Globals.h
16   extern double cylinder_center_position_x;
17   extern double cylinder_width;
18   extern double cylinder_center_position_y;
19   extern double cylinder_height;
20   extern int push_pull;
21   extern int is_testing;
22   // DONE: reference the control variable for "info" simulation
23   extern int is_info_simulation;
24   // DONE: reference the intermediate stage period
25   extern double inter_period;
26   extern double ball0_time;
27   extern double ball0_delta_speed;
28   extern double ball0_delta_angle;
29
30
31   template <typename T>
32   T MessageQueue<T>::receive()
33   {
34
35       std::unique_lock<std::mutex> uLock(_mutex);       // needs unique_lock because the lock
36       // will be temporarily unlocked inside wait
37       _cond.wait(uLock, [this] { return !_queue.empty(); });     // enter the wait state,
38       // release the lock and resume if new data is available
39
40       T msg = std::move(_queue.back());
41       _queue.pop_back();
42
43       //std::cout << "Message " << msg  << " has been received from the Ball msg queue"
44       // << std::endl;
45
46       return msg;
47   }
48
49   template <typename T>
50   void MessageQueue<T>::send(T&& msg)
51   {
```

```cpp
52
53        std::lock_guard<std::mutex> uLock(_mutex);
54
55        //std::cout << "Message " <<  msg << " has been sent to the Ball msg queue"
56        // << std::endl;
57
58        _queue.push_back(std::move(msg));
59        _cond.notify_one();
60
61    }
62
63    template <typename T>
64    int MessageQueue<T>::getSize()
65    {
66        std::lock_guard<std::mutex> uLock(_mutex);
67        return _queue.size();
68    }
69
70    // helper function declaration
71    double distanceToPoint(double x1, double y1, double x2, double y2);
72    bool squareCircleCollision(double x1, double y1, double w1, double h1,
73                               double x2, double y2, double r2);
74    bool circleCircleCollision(double x1, double y1, double r1,
75                               double x2, double y2, double r2);
76    void resolveCollision(double& posX, double& posY, double& velX, double& velY,
77                          double speed, double mass, double radius,
78                          double& otherX, double& otherY,
79                          double& otherVx, double& otherVy,
80                          double otherSpeed, double otherM, double otherR, bool isWall,
81                          double coef_e, double coef_G);
82
83    Ball::Ball()
84    {
85        _type = ObjectType::objectBall;
86        _radius = 0;
87        _velX = 0;
88        _velY = 0;
89        _speed = 0;
90        _shutDown = false;
91        _ball_gravity = 0;
92        _gas_mode = false;
93        _coef_e = 0;
94        _coef_G = 0;
95        // DONE: initialize variables of "info" simulation
96        _info_stage = 0;
97        _propagation_time = NULL;
98    }
99
100    // DONE: set/get "info" simulation data
101    void Ball::setInfoStage(int stage) {
102        std::lock_guard<std::mutex> lock(_mutex);
103        _info_stage = stage;
104    }
105
106    int Ball::getInfoStage() {
```

```cpp
        std::lock_guard<std::mutex> lock(_mutex);
        return _info_stage;
    }

    // DONE: set/get time
    void Ball::setPropagationTime(std::time_t time) {
        std::lock_guard<std::mutex> lock(_mutex);
        _propagation_time = time;
    }

    std::time_t Ball::getPropagationTime() {
        std::lock_guard<std::mutex> lock(_mutex);
        return _propagation_time;
    }

    void Ball::setSpecificDirection(double speed, double angle)
    {
        // set velocity
        double vx, vy;
        double pi = acos(-1);
        vx = speed * cos(angle * 2 * pi / 360);
        vy = -speed * sin(angle * 2 * pi / 360);
        setVelocity(vx, vy);
    }

    void Ball::setRandomDirection(double speed)
    {
        // pick angle at random and set direction of the ball
        double angle;
        std::random_device rd;
        std::mt19937 generator(rd());
        std::array<double, 5> intervals{ -60.0, 60.0, 120.0, 240.0, 360.0 };
        std::array<double, 4> weights{ 1.0, 1.0, 1.0, 1.0 };
        std::piecewise_constant_distribution<double>
            distribution(intervals.begin(), intervals.end(), weights.begin());
        angle = distribution(generator);

        std::cout << "Angle " << angle << std::endl;

        // set velocity
        setSpecificDirection(speed, angle);
    }

    bool Ball::dataIsAvailable()
    {
        return (_msgQueue.getSize() > 0);
    }

    CollisionData Ball::receiveMsg()
    {
        return _msgQueue.receive();
    }

    bool Ball::getShutdown()
    {
```

```cpp
162        return _shutDown;
163    }
164
165    void Ball::setShutdown()
166    {
167        _shutDown = true;
168    }
169
170    // implement the virtual function that will execute a member function into a thread
171    void Ball::simulate()
172    {
173        // Start a thread with the member function "play" and the object "this"
174        // Add the created thread into the _threads vector of parent class (using
175        // emplace_back which means move semantics)
176        _threads.emplace_back(std::thread(&Ball::play, this));
177    }
178
179    // function which is executed in athread
180    void Ball::play()
181    {
182
183        // print Ball id and thread id
184        std::unique_lock<std::mutex> uLock(mtxCout);
185        std::cout << "Ball::simulate Ball _id=" << getID() << "  thread id=" <<
186        std::this_thread::get_id() << std::endl;
187        uLock.unlock();
188
189        long count = 0;
190
191        // initialize variables
192
193        // define cycle duration (to update ball position and check cylinder)
194        int cycleDuration = 10;  // duration of a single simulation cycle in ms
195
196        // init stop watch
197        std::chrono::time_point<std::chrono::system_clock> lastUpdate, simBegin;
198        lastUpdate = std::chrono::system_clock::now();
199        simBegin = std::chrono::system_clock::now();
200
201        // infinite simulation loop
202        while (!getShutdown())
203        {
204            // compute time difference to stop watch (in ms)
205            auto timeSinceLastUpdate = std::chrono::duration_cast<std::chrono
206                ::milliseconds>(std::chrono::system_clock::now() -
207                    lastUpdate).count();
208
209            // if past cycle time, update position and check cylinder
210            if (timeSinceLastUpdate >= cycleDuration)
211            {
212
213                // reset stop watch for next cycle
214                lastUpdate = std::chrono::system_clock::now();
215
216                // calc next position
```

```cpp
        double velX, velY, nextX, nextY;
        double posX, posY, dx, dy;
        getVelocity(velX, velY);
        getPosition(posX, posY);

        dx = velX * (timeSinceLastUpdate / 1000.0); // dx = Vx * dt

        // calc gravity acceleration effect
        dy = velY * (timeSinceLastUpdate / 1000.0) +
            0.5 * _ball_gravity * pow(timeSinceLastUpdate / 1000.0, 2.0);

        double dVy = _ball_gravity * (timeSinceLastUpdate / 1000.0);  // dVy = Ay*dt


        // calc gravitational/force field
        // F = G * m1 * m2 / r^2
        // Gf = G * m2 / r^2
        int thisBallId = getID();

        double Gf = 0.0;     // field
        double Gfx = 0.0;
        double Gfy = 0.0;
        double coef_G = getG();
        double dGVx = 0.0;
        double dGVy = 0.0;

        if (coef_G > 0 || coef_G < 0)
        {
            for (auto ball : _balls)
            {
                int otherBallId = ball->getID();
                if (thisBallId != otherBallId)
                {
                    double otherX, otherY;
                    ball->getPosition(otherX, otherY);

                    double m2 = ball->getMass();
                    double r = distanceToPoint(posX + dx/2, posY + dy/2,
                        otherX, otherY);
                    Gf = coef_G * m2 / (r * r);
                    double angle = atan2(otherY - posY - dy/2, otherX - posX -dx/2);
                    Gfx += Gf * cos(angle);
                    Gfy += Gf * sin(angle);
                }
            }

            // calc gravitational acceleration effect
            dx += 0.5 * Gfx * pow(timeSinceLastUpdate / 1000.0, 2.0);
            dy += 0.5 * Gfy * pow(timeSinceLastUpdate / 1000.0, 2.0);

            dGVx = Gfx * (timeSinceLastUpdate / 1000.0);   // dV = A*dt
            dGVy = Gfy * (timeSinceLastUpdate / 1000.0);
        }

        // update velocity before entering the collision
```

```cpp
272             velX += dGVx;
273             velY += dVy + dGVy;
274
275             // update delta_speed in ball0
276             if ( _id == _balls.at(0)->getID() &&
277                 (std::chrono::duration_cast<std::chrono::milliseconds>
278                 (std::chrono::system_clock::now() - simBegin).count() > ball0_time) &&
279                 ball0_time != 0 && is_testing == 1) {
280                 velX += ball0_delta_speed * cos(ball0_delta_angle * acos(-1) / 180);
281                 velY += ball0_delta_speed * (-1.0) * sin(ball0_delta_angle *
282                     acos(-1) / 180);
283                 ball0_time = 0;
284             }
285
286             setVelocity(velX, velY);
287
288             // print time to orbit
289             if (_id == _balls.at(0)->getID() &&
290                 ball0_time != 0 && getSpeed() < 1.0 && is_testing == 1) {
291                 auto time = std::chrono::duration_cast<std::chrono::milliseconds>
292                     (std::chrono::system_clock::now() - simBegin).count();
293                 double x1, y1, x2, y2;
294                 _balls.at(0)->getPosition(x1, y1);
295                 _balls.at(1)->getPosition(x2, y2);
296                 double orbit = distanceToPoint(x1, y1, x2, y2);
297                 uLock.lock();
298                 std::cout << "speed: " << getSpeed() << " time: " << time <<
299                     " orbit:" << std::setprecision(6) << orbit << std::endl;
300                 uLock.unlock();
301             }
302
303             // next position
304             nextX = posX + dx;
305             nextY = posY + dy;
306
307             // check if ball has colided
308             bool hasCollided = false;
309
310             // process ball with wall collision
311             // m0*v0i + m1*v1i = m0*v0f + m1*v1f
312             // Ec0i + Ec1i >= Ec0f + Ec1f
313             for (auto wall : _walls) {
314
315                 // process piston->ball collision (the piston moves in y axis):
316                 if (wall->getWallType() == WallType::piston)
317                 {
318                     // begin of piston critical section
319                     std::unique_lock<std::mutex> pLock(wall->wall_mutex);
320
321                     // if ball is inside the piston: flag the collision
322                     if (checkWallCollision(nextX, nextY, wall)) {
323
324                         hasCollided = true;
325
326                         double otherVx, otherVy;
```

```cpp
            wall->getVelocity(otherVx, otherVy);
            double x, y, w, h;
            wall->getPosition(x, y);
            wall->getSize(w, h);

            double velCollisionGas = velY;

            double otherX, otherY;
            otherX = posX;  // like collision with ball at same x coordinate
            otherY = y;

            double speed = getSpeed();
            double otherSpeed = wall->getSpeed();

            double mass = _mass;
            double otherM = wall->getMass();

            // limit pistom movement to the cylinder
            if (otherY <= (cylinder_center_position_y -
                cylinder_height * 0.5) * 1.001)
            {
                otherM = 1e100;

            }

            double radius = _radius;
            double otherR = h / 2;     // it is like a collision with a ball
            // at the same x coordinate, with r = h/2

            double coef_e = getCoefRestitution();

            resolveCollision(posX, posY, velX, velY,
                             speed, mass, radius,
                             otherX, otherY, otherVx, otherVy,
                             otherSpeed, otherM, otherR, false,
                             coef_e, coef_G);

            // Two models of simulation: in the gas mode, the piston is
            // processed in main
            if (!_gas_mode)
            {
                // update positions and velocities
                wall->setVelocity(0, otherVy);
                wall->setPosition(x, otherY);

                setVelocity(velX, velY);
                setPosition(posX, posY);

            }
            else
            {
                // update ball position and velocity
                setVelocity(velX, velY);
                setPosition(posX, posY);
```

```cpp
                            // msg to main, to update piston:
                            _msgQueue.send({ CollisionType::pistonCollision,
                                           velCollisionGas - velY });
                    }

                }

            // end of piston critical section
            pLock.unlock();

            if (hasCollided) {
                break;
            }

        }

        // process collision with laterals
        if (wall->getWallType() == WallType::lateral)
        {

            // if there is a collision, change ball direction
            if (checkWallCollision(nextX, nextY, wall)) {

                //std::cout << "ball with lateral collision" << std::endl;

                hasCollided = true;

                double otherVx, otherVy;  // wall
                otherVx = 0;
                otherVy = 0;
                double x, y, w, h;
                wall->getPosition(x, y);
                wall->getSize(w, h);

                double coef_e = getCoefRestitution();

                double otherX, otherY;
                otherX = x;  // like collision with ball at same x coordinate
                otherY = posY;

                double speed = getSpeed();
                double otherSpeed = 0;

                double mass = _mass;
                double otherM = 1e100;

                double radius = _radius;
                double otherR = w / 2;    // it is like a collision with a ball
                // at the same y coordinate, with r = w/2

                resolveCollision(posX, posY, velX, velY,
                                 speed, mass, radius,
                                 otherX, otherY, otherVx, otherVy,
                                 otherSpeed, otherM, otherR, true,
                                 coef_e, coef_G);
```

```cpp
            // update velocity
            setVelocity(velX, velY);

            // update position
            setPosition(posX, posY);

            break;

        }

    }

    // process collision with bottom
    if (wall->getWallType() == WallType::bottom)
    {

        if (checkWallCollision(nextX, nextY, wall)) {

            //std::cout << "ball with bottom collision" << std::endl;

            hasCollided = true;

            double otherVx, otherVy;  // bottom
            otherVx = 0;
            otherVy = 0;
            double x, y, w, h;
            wall->getPosition(x, y);
            wall->getSize(w, h);

            double coef_e = getCoefRestitution();

            double otherX, otherY;
            otherX = posX;  // like collision with ball at same x coordinate
            otherY = y;

            double speed = getSpeed();
            double otherSpeed = 0;

            double mass = _mass;
            double otherM = 1e100;

            double radius = _radius;
            double otherR = h / 2;    // it is like a collision with a ball
            // at the same x coordinate, with r = h/2

            resolveCollision(posX, posY, velX, velY,
                             speed, mass, radius,
                             otherX, otherY, otherVx, otherVy,
                             otherSpeed, otherM, otherR, true,
                             coef_e, coef_G);

            // Adjust ball velocity to aprox temperature effect of bottom
            if (wall->getWallType() == WallType::bottom) {
                if (abs(velY) < 1.0 * wall->getHeat())
```

```cpp
492                         {
493                             velY = -1.0 * wall->getHeat();
494                         }
495                     }

497                     // update velocity
498                     setVelocity(velX, velY);
499                     // update position
500                     setPosition(posX, posY);

502                     break;

504                 }

506             }

508         } // eof ball-wall collision


511         // process ball with ball collisions
512         // m0*v0i + m1*v1i = m0*v0f + m1*v1f
513         // Ec0i + Ec1i >= Ec0f + Ec1f
514         if (!hasCollided)
515         {
516             int thisBallId = getID();
517             for (auto ball : _balls)
518             {

520                 int otherBallId = ball->getID();

522                 if (thisBallId != otherBallId &&
523                     checkBallCollision(nextX, nextY, ball))
524                 {
525                     //uLock.lock();
526                     //std::cout << "ball:" << thisBallId << " with ball:" <<
527                     //    otherBallId <<  " collision" << std::endl;
528                     //uLock.unlock();

530                     // if there is a collision, change ball direction
531                     // elastic collision

533                     hasCollided = true;

535                     // DONE: process the transmission
536                     if (is_info_simulation == 1) {

538                         time_t timer;
539                         time(&timer);
540                         // transmission to other ball
541                         // if other ball is unaware, turn aware (stage 1)
542                         if (ball->getInfoStage() == 0 && getInfoStage() == 1) {

544                             ball->setInfoStage(1);
545                             ball->setPropagationTime(timer);
546
```

```cpp
547                        // transmission from other ball
548                        // if this ball is unaware, turn aware (stage 1)
549                        } else if (getInfoStage() == 0 && ball->getInfoStage() == 1) {
550
551                            setInfoStage(1);
552                            setPropagationTime(timer);
553
554                        }
555                    }
556
557                    double otherX, otherY;
558                    ball->getPosition(otherX, otherY);
559
560                    double otherVx, otherVy;
561                    ball->getVelocity(otherVx, otherVy);
562
563                    // approx. do not use all dGV (collide first)
564                    velX = velX - 0.5 * dGVx;
565                    velY = velY - 0.5 * dGVy;
566
567                    double speed = sqrt(pow(velX, 2.0) + pow(velY, 2.0));
568                    double otherSpeed = ball->getSpeed();
569
570                    double mass = getMass();
571                    double otherM = ball->getMass();
572
573                    double radius = getRadius();
574                    double otherR = ball->getRadius();
575
576                    double coef_e = getCoefRestitution();
577
578
579                    resolveCollision(posX, posY, velX, velY,
580                                     speed, mass, radius,
581                                     otherX, otherY, otherVx, otherVy,
582                                     otherSpeed, otherM, otherR, false,
583                                     coef_e, coef_G);
584
585                    // update velocities
586                    setVelocity(velX, velY);
587                    ball->setVelocity(otherVx, otherVy);
588
589                    // update positions
590                    setPosition(posX, posY);
591                    ball->setPosition(otherX, otherY);
592
593                }
594
595            }
596
597        } // eof new ball-ball collision
598
599        // if has not colided, just update position (velocity has been updated)
600        if (!hasCollided) {
601            setPosition(nextX, nextY);
```

```cpp
            }

        } // eof cycle


        // DONE: process aware stage of "info" simmulation
        if (getInfoStage() == 1) {
            time_t timer;
            time(&timer);
            if (difftime(timer, getPropagationTime()) > inter_period) {
                setInfoStage(2);
            }
        }


        // sleep at every iteration to reduce CPU usage
        std::this_thread::sleep_for(std::chrono::milliseconds(1));

    } // eof simulation loop


    // print Ball id and thread id
    uLock.lock();
    std::cout << "Ball::simulate closing Ball _id=" << getID() << "  thread id=" <<
        std::this_thread::get_id() << std::endl;
    uLock.unlock();
}

// Verify and process the collision of the ball with the cylinder walls
bool Ball::checkWallCollision(double nextX, double nextY, std::shared_ptr<Wall> wall)
{
    double x, y, w, h;
    bool collision = false;

    wall->getPosition(x, y);
    wall->getSize(w, h);
    collision = squareCircleCollision(x, y, w, h, nextX, nextY, _radius);

    return collision;
}

// Verify and process the collision of the ball with the cylinder walls
bool Ball::checkBallCollision(double nextX, double nextY, std::shared_ptr<Ball> ball)
{
    double x, y, r;
    bool collision = false;

    ball->getPosition(x, y);
    r = ball->getRadius();
    collision = circleCircleCollision(nextX, nextY, _radius, x, y, r);

    return collision;
}

// verify collision between square x1,y1,w1,h1 and circle x2,y2,r2
```

```cpp
bool squareCircleCollision(double x1, double y1, double w1, double h1,
                           double x2, double y2, double r2)
{
    double closestX, closestY;
    bool collision = false;

    // find the closest x coordinate of the wall to the circle
    if (x1 + w1 * 0.5 < x2 - r2) { closestX = x1 + w1 * 0.5; }
    else if (x1 - w1 * 0.5 > x2 + r2) { closestX = x1 - w1 * 0.5; }
    else { closestX = x2; }

    // find the closest y coordinate of the wall to the circle
    if (y1 + h1 * 0.5 < y2 - r2) { closestY = y1 + h1 * 0.5; }
    else if (y1 - h1 * 0.5 > y2 + r2) { closestY = y1 - h1 * 0.5; }
    else { closestY = y2; }

    if (distanceToPoint(x2, y2, closestX, closestY) < (r2 - 1e-3)) {
        collision = true;
    }

    return collision;
}

// verify collision between circle x1,y1,r1 and circle x2,y2,r2
bool circleCircleCollision(double x1, double y1, double r1,
                           double x2, double y2, double r2)
{
    double distance;
    bool collision;

    distance = distanceToPoint(x1, y1, x2, y2);
    collision = (distance < (r1 + r2 - 1e-3));

    return collision;
}

double distanceToPoint(double x1, double y1, double x2, double y2)
{
    double distance;

    distance = sqrt(pow(x1 - x2, 2.0) + pow(y1 - y2, 2.0));

    return distance;
}

// resolve collision elastic
void resolveCollision(double& posX, double& posY, double& velX, double& velY,
                      double speed, double mass, double radius,
                      double& otherX, double& otherY, double& otherVx, double& otherVy,
                      double otherSpeed, double otherM, double otherR, bool isWall,
                      double coef_e, double coef_G)
{

    if (mass == 0 || otherM == 0)
    {
```

```cpp
            std::cout << "Error: mass is zero!" << std::endl;
            return;
        }

        double angleCol = atan2(otherY - posY, otherX - posX);
        double direction = atan2(velY, velX);
        double otherDirection = atan2(otherVy, otherVx);

        double new_xspeed = speed * cos(direction - angleCol);
        double new_yspeed = speed * sin(direction - angleCol);

        double new_xspeedOther = otherSpeed * cos(otherDirection - angleCol);
        double new_yspeedOther = otherSpeed * sin(otherDirection - angleCol);

        double final_xspeed = ((mass - coef_e * otherM) * new_xspeed +
            (otherM + coef_e * otherM) * new_xspeedOther) / (mass + otherM);
        double final_xspeedOther = ((mass + coef_e * mass) * new_xspeed +
            (otherM - coef_e * mass) * new_xspeedOther) / (mass + otherM);
        double final_yspeed = new_yspeed;
        double final_yspeedOther = new_yspeedOther;

        double cosAngle = cos(angleCol);
        double sinAngle = sin(angleCol);

        double newVelX, newVelY;
        newVelX = cosAngle * final_xspeed - sinAngle * final_yspeed;
        newVelY = sinAngle * final_xspeed + cosAngle * final_yspeed;

        double newOtherVelX, newOtherVelY;
        newOtherVelX = cosAngle * final_xspeedOther - sinAngle * final_yspeedOther;
        newOtherVelY = sinAngle * final_xspeedOther + cosAngle * final_yspeedOther;

        // get the minimum translation distance to push balls apart after intersecting
        struct Position {
            double x;
            double y;
            double length() {
                return sqrt(pow(x, 2.0) + pow(y, 2.0));
            }
        } pos1, pos2, posDiff, mtd;

        pos1.x = posX;
        pos1.y = posY;
        pos2.x = otherX;
        pos2.y = otherY;
        posDiff.x = pos1.x - pos2.x;
        posDiff.y = pos1.y - pos2.y;

        double d = posDiff.length();
        double k = (((radius + otherR) - d) / d);
        mtd.x = posDiff.x * k;
        mtd.y = posDiff.y * k;

        double im = 1 / mass;
        double imOther = 1 / otherM;
```

```
        // push-pull them apart based off their mass, if the flag was set
        if (push_pull == 1 ) {
            pos1.x = pos1.x + mtd.x * (im / (im + imOther));
            pos1.y = pos1.y + mtd.y * (im / (im + imOther));
            pos2.x = pos2.x - mtd.x * (imOther / (im + imOther));
            pos2.y = pos2.y - mtd.y * (imOther / (im + imOther));


            // Process ball with wall collision generated by the pushing balls apart
            if ((pos1.x + radius >= cylinder_center_position_x + cylinder_width / 2) ||
                (pos1.x - radius <= cylinder_center_position_x - cylinder_width / 2))
            {
                newVelX = -1.0 * newVelX;
            }

            if ((pos1.y + radius >= cylinder_center_position_y + cylinder_height / 2) ||
                (pos1.y - radius <= cylinder_center_position_y - cylinder_height / 2))
            {
                newVelY = -1.0 * newVelY;
            }


            // if other is a wall of the cylinder, do not process (is not valid)
            if (((pos2.x + otherR >= cylinder_center_position_x + cylinder_width / 2) ||
                (pos2.x - otherR <= cylinder_center_position_x - cylinder_width / 2)) &&
                !isWall)
            {
                newOtherVelX = -1.0 * newOtherVelX;
            }

            // if other is a wall of the cylinder, do not process (is not valid)
            if (((pos2.y + otherR >= cylinder_center_position_y + cylinder_height / 2) ||
                (pos2.y - otherR <= cylinder_center_position_y - cylinder_height / 2)) &&
                !isWall)
            {
                newOtherVelY = -1.0 * newOtherVelY;

            }

        }

    velX = newVelX;
    velY = newVelY;

    posX = pos1.x;
    posY = pos1.y;

    otherVx = newOtherVelX;
    otherVy = newOtherVelY;

    otherX = pos2.x;
    otherY = pos2.y;
    }
```

```cpp
#include "Wall.h"

Wall::Wall()
{
    _type = ObjectType::objectWall;
    _wallType = WallType::lateral;
    _width = 0;
    _height = 0;
    _temp = 0;
}

void  Wall::setSize(double w, double h)
{
    _width = w;
    _height = h;
}

void  Wall::getSize(double& w, double& h)
{
    w = _width;
    h = _height;
}

void Wall::setHeat(double ht)
{
    std::lock_guard<std::mutex> lock(_mutex);
    _temp = ht;
}

double Wall::getHeat()
{
    std::lock_guard<std::mutex> lock(_mutex);
    return _temp;
}
```

```cpp
1    #include <iostream>
2    #include <iomanip>
3
4    #include "Ball.h"
5    #include "Wall.h"
6
7    // Variables defined at Globals.h
8    extern double gas_mode;
9    extern double cylinder_center_position_x;
10   extern double cylinder_width;
11   extern double cylinder_center_position_y;
12   extern double cylinder_height;
13   extern double wall_width;
14   extern double piston_mass;
15   extern double piston_gravity;
16   extern double coef_rest;
17   extern int is_testing;
18   extern double ball0_time;
19   extern double ball0_delta_speed;
20
21
22   void processPiston(std::shared_ptr<Wall> piston, std::shared_ptr<Wall> bottom,
23       std::vector<std::shared_ptr<Ball>> balls, bool& finish)
24   {
25
26       // Set to piston dynamics
27       long pistoncollisions = 0;
28       double upForce = 0.0;
29       double mv = 0.0;
30       double avgUpForce = 0.0;
31       double downForce = 0.0;     // for testing
32       downForce = piston_gravity * piston_mass;
33       double pistonVel = 0.0;
34       int cycleDuration = 10;   // define cycle duration (ms) to calc up force
35       bool gasMode = (gas_mode > 0);
36       double temp = 0;
37
38
39       // init stop watch
40       std::chrono::time_point<std::chrono::system_clock> lastUpdate;
41       lastUpdate = std::chrono::system_clock::now();
42
43       auto f0 = [balls, bottom, cycleDuration, gasMode, &avgUpForce, &downForce,
44           &temp, &finish]()
45       {
46           long simTime = 0;
47           while (!finish) {
48               std::this_thread::sleep_for(std::chrono::milliseconds(1000));
49               // count balls inside piston (testing)
50               int count = 0;
51               for (auto ball : balls)
```

```cpp
52              {
53                  double x, y;
54                  ball->getPosition(x, y);
55                  if (x > cylinder_center_position_x - cylinder_width * 0.5 && x  <
56                      cylinder_center_position_x + cylinder_width * 0.5 &&
57                      y > cylinder_center_position_y - cylinder_height * 0.5 && y <
58                      cylinder_center_position_y + cylinder_height * 0.5)
59                  {
60                      count++;
61                  }
62                  else {
63                      ball->setShutdown();
64                  }
65              }
66
67              std::unique_lock<std::mutex> uLock(bottom->mtxCout);
68              std::cout << "Time:" << simTime << "\t";
69              std::cout << "balls:" << count << "    ";
70
71              if (gasMode) {
72                  std::cout << "gas avg(1.0s) up force : " << std::fixed <<
73                      std::setprecision(2) << abs(avgUpForce) << "  \t";
74                  std::cout << "piston down force: " << std::setprecision(2) <<
75                      downForce << " \t";
76              }
77
78              temp = bottom->getHeat();
79              std::cout << "~temp(bottom) : " << std::setprecision(2) << temp <<
80                  std::endl;
81
82              // print orbit distance
83              if (ball0_delta_speed != 0 && is_testing == 1 && ball0_time == 0) {
84                  double x1, y1, x2, y2;
85                  balls.at(0)->getPosition(x1, y1);
86                  balls.at(1)->getPosition(x2, y2);
87                  double orbit = sqrt(pow(x1 - x2, 2.0) + pow(y1 - y2, 2.0));
88                  std::cout << "speed: " << std::setprecision(6) <<
89                      balls.at(0)->getSpeed() << "  >>> orbit:" << orbit <<
90                      " <<<\n" << std::endl;
91              }
92
93              uLock.unlock();
94
95              simTime++;
96          }
97      };
98
99      std::thread t1(f0);          // thread for monitoring and testing
100
101
102      while (!finish)
103      {
104
105          // compute time difference (in ms)
106          auto timeSinceLastUpdate =
```

```cpp
107            std::chrono::duration_cast<std::chrono::milliseconds>
108            (std::chrono::system_clock::now() - lastUpdate).count();
109
110        // Receive and process msg from balls about a collision with the piston
111        for (auto ball : balls)
112        {
113            while (ball->dataIsAvailable())
114            {
115                //std::cout << "Main: ball msg available" << std::endl;
116                CollisionData msg = ball->receiveMsg();
117                CollisionType colType = msg.type;
118                double velocity = msg.velY;     // downward is positve
119                switch (colType) {
120                case CollisionType::bottomCollision:
121                    //std::cout << "ball-bottom collision" << std::endl;
122                    break;
123                case CollisionType::pistonCollision:
124                    //std::cout << "*gas* ball-piston collision " << "mv: "
125                    //<< mv << std::endl;
126                    pistoncollisions++;
127                    mv += ball->getMass() * velocity;     // change in momentum
128                    break;
129                }
130            }
131
132        }
133
134
135        // Process piston dymamics
136        if (timeSinceLastUpdate > cycleDuration) {
137
138            // begin of critical section
139            std::unique_lock<std::mutex> pLock(piston->wall_mutex);
140
141            // F * t = m * v
142            upForce = mv / (timeSinceLastUpdate / 1000.0);
143            avgUpForce = avgUpForce + upForce / (1000.0 / cycleDuration) - avgUpForce /
144                (1000.0 / cycleDuration);     // 1000ms average (for printing)
145
146            double posX, posY;
147            double velX, velY;
148            double acceleration;
149
150            piston->getPosition(posX, posY);
151            piston->getVelocity(velX, velY);
152
153            // F = m * a
154            acceleration = (upForce + downForce) / (piston_mass + 1e-10);  // downward =
155            // positive; prevent overflow
156
157            // calc piston position  (x - x0) = vo * t + 1/2 * a * t^2
158            posY = posY + velY * (timeSinceLastUpdate / 1000.0) +
159                0.5 * acceleration * pow(timeSinceLastUpdate / 1000.0, 2.0);     // approx;
160
161            // piston velocity for next cycle
```

```cpp
162                 pistonVel = velY + acceleration * (timeSinceLastUpdate / 1000.0);
163
164             // piston at the top: no velocity upward
165             if (posY < (cylinder_center_position_y - cylinder_height * 0.5))
166             {
167                 if (pistonVel < 0) pistonVel = -coef_rest * pistonVel;
168                 posY = cylinder_center_position_y - cylinder_height * 0.5;
169             }
170             // piston at the bottom: no velocity downward
171             else if (posY > (cylinder_center_position_y +
172                 cylinder_height * 0.5 - wall_width))
173             {
174                 if (pistonVel > 0) pistonVel = -coef_rest * pistonVel;
175                 posY = cylinder_center_position_y +
176                     cylinder_height * 0.5 - wall_width;
177             }
178
179             // update piston
180             piston->setPosition(posX, posY);
181             piston->setVelocity(0.0, pistonVel);
182
183             // end of critical section
184             pLock.unlock();
185
186             // reset for next cycle
187             pistoncollisions = 0;
188             mv = 0.0;
189
190             // reset stop watch for next cycle
191             lastUpdate = std::chrono::system_clock::now();
192
193
194         } // eof cycle computations
195
196         //sleep at every iteration to reduce CPU usage
197         std::this_thread::sleep_for(std::chrono::milliseconds(1));
198
199     } // eof while loop
200
201
202     t1.join(); // it will close because it is monitoring the finish flag
203
204 }
205
```

```cpp
1
2    #include <iostream>
3    #include <iomanip>
4    #include <fstream>
5    #include <string>
6    #include <thread>
7    #include <vector>
8    #include <array>
9    #include <random>
10   #include <ctime>
11   #include <vector>
12
13   // Download the SDL2-devel-...zip library from libsdl.org
14   // Manual installation:
15   // C/C++ -> General -> AdditionalIncludeDirectories ->
16   // <path>\SDL2-devel-2.0.10-VC\SDL2-2.0.10\include;%(AdditionalIncludeDirectories)
17   // Linker -> General -> AdditionalLibraryDirectories ->
18   // <path>\SDL2-devel-2.0.10-VC\SDL2-2.0.10\lib\x86;%(AdditionalLibraryDirectories)
19   // Linker->Input->AdditionalDependencies->SDL2.lib;SDL2main.lib;%(AdditionalDependencies)
20   // Linker -> Subsystem -> Console (/SUBSYSTEM:CONSOLE)
21   // Copy the <path>\SDL2-devel-2.0.10-VC\SDL2-2.0.10\lib\x86\SDL2.dll to the project folder
22   #include <SDL2/SDL.h>
23
24   #include "Ball.h"
25   #include "Wall.h"
26   #include "Piston.h"
27   #include "Globals.h"
28
29   // The window we will be rendering to
30   std::shared_ptr<SDL_Window> gWindow = nullptr;
31
32   // The window renderer
33   std::shared_ptr<SDL_Renderer> gRenderer = nullptr;
34
35   // Starts up SDL and creates window
36   bool initRenderer();
37
38   // Free media and shut down SDL
39   void closeRenderer();
40
41   // Draw circle using midpoint circle algorithm
42   void drawCircle(std::shared_ptr<SDL_Renderer> gRenderer,
43                   int32_t centreX, int32_t centreY, int32_t radius);
44
45   // Load parameters from file
46   bool chooseSimulations();
47   bool loadParametersFromFile();
48   void printParameters();
49
50   // Create objects;
51   void createObjects(std::vector<std::shared_ptr<Wall>>& walls,
```

```cpp
                        std::shared_ptr<Wall>& piston, std::shared_ptr<Wall>& bottom,
                        std::vector<std::shared_ptr<Ball>>& balls);

// Render objects
void renderBall(std::shared_ptr<Ball> ball);
void renderWalls(std::vector<std::shared_ptr<Wall>> walls);


/* Main function */
int main(int argc, char* args[]) // needs argc and args[] for the SDL
{

    // Simulation objects
    std::vector<std::shared_ptr<Wall>> walls;
    std::shared_ptr<Wall> piston;
    std::shared_ptr<Wall> bottom;
    std::vector<std::shared_ptr<Ball>> balls;


    // Choose simulations
    if (!chooseSimulations())
        return 0;

    // set min value for "e"
    //if (coef_rest < 1e-6) {
    //    coef_rest = 1e-6;
    //}

    // create the objects
    createObjects(walls, piston, bottom, balls);

    if (balls.size() >= 1 && is_testing > 0) {
        // set for testing
        balls.at(0)->setSpecificDirection(ball0_speed, ball0_vel_angle);
        if (ball0_x != -1) {
            double x, y;
            balls.at(0)->getPosition(x, y);
            balls.at(0)->setPosition(ball0_x, y);
        }
        if (ball0_y != -1) {
            double x, y;
            balls.at(0)->getPosition(x, y);
            balls.at(0)->setPosition(x, ball0_y);
        }
        if (ball0_radius != -1) {
            balls.at(0)->setRadius(ball0_radius);
        }
        if (ball0_mass != -1) {
            balls.at(0)->setMass(ball0_mass);
        }
    }


    if (balls.size() >= 2 && is_testing > 0) {
        // set for testing
```

```cpp
        balls.at(1)->setSpecificDirection(ball1_speed, ball1_vel_angle);
        if (ball1_x != -1) {
            double x, y;
            balls.at(1)->getPosition(x, y);
            balls.at(1)->setPosition(ball1_x, y);
        }
        if (ball1_y != -1) {
            double x, y;
            balls.at(1)->getPosition(x, y);
            balls.at(1)->setPosition(x, ball1_y);
        }
        if (ball1_radius != -1) {
            balls.at(1)->setRadius(ball1_radius);
        }
        if (ball1_mass != -1) {
            balls.at(1)->setMass(ball1_mass);
        }
    }

    // DONE: Set the balls for "info" simmulation
    if (is_info_simulation > 0) {
        // set the first ball with the aware stage
        balls.at(0)->setInfoStage(1);
        // set the first ball with the time
        time_t time_now;
        time(&time_now);
        balls.at(0)->setPropagationTime(time_now);
    }

    // msg for stopping the threads
    bool finish = false;

    // process piston dynamics
    std::thread t1(processPiston, piston, bottom, std::ref(balls), std::ref(finish));

    // Start up SDL and create window
    if (!initRenderer())
    {
        std::cout << "Failed to initialize!" << std::endl;
    }
    else
    {
        // wait before starting
        std::this_thread::sleep_for(std::chrono::milliseconds(100));

        // simulate
        for (auto ball : balls)
        {
            ball->simulate();
        }

        // initialize variables
        bool quit = false; // loop flag
        int tempKey = 0;
```

```cpp
// Main loop
while (!quit)
{

    SDL_Event e; // Event handler

    // Handle key cylinder events on queue
    while (SDL_PollEvent(&e) != 0)
    {
        // User requests quit
        if (e.type == SDL_QUIT)
        {
            quit = true;
        }

        // adjust temp at bottom
        if (e.type == SDL_KEYDOWN && e.key.repeat == 0)
        {
            switch (e.key.keysym.sym)
            {
            case SDLK_LEFT:
                tempKey = -1;
                break;
            case SDLK_RIGHT:
                tempKey = +1;
                break;
            default:
                break;
            }
        }

        if (e.type == SDL_KEYUP && e.key.repeat == 0)
        {
            switch (e.key.keysym.sym)
            {
            case SDLK_LEFT:
                if(tempKey < 0)
                    tempKey = 0;
                break;
            case SDLK_RIGHT:
                if(tempKey > 0)
                    tempKey = 0;
                break;
            default:
                break;
            }
        }

    }

    // update temp
    if (tempKey == +1) {
        double temp = bottom->getHeat();
        if (temp < bottom_temp_max) {
            temp++;
```

```cpp
217                     bottom->setHeat(temp);
218                 }
219             }
220             if (tempKey == -1) {
221                 double temp = bottom->getHeat();
222                 if (temp > bottom_temp_min) {
223                     temp--;
224                     bottom->setHeat(temp);
225                 }
226             }
227
228             // Clear screen
229             if (background_color == 1) {
230                 SDL_SetRenderDrawColor(gRenderer.get(), 0xFF, 0xFF, 0xFF, 0xFF);
231             }
232             else {
233                 SDL_SetRenderDrawColor(gRenderer.get(), 0x00, 0x00, 0x00, 0xFF);
234             }
235             SDL_RenderClear(gRenderer.get());
236
237             // Render ball
238             for (auto ball : balls)
239             {
240                 renderBall(ball);
241             }
242
243             // Render walls
244             renderWalls(walls);
245
246             // Update screen
247             SDL_RenderPresent(gRenderer.get());
248
249         } // eof main loop
250
251
252         // ask ball:simulate to terminate
253         for (auto ball : balls) {
254             ball->setShutdown();
255         }
256
257     }
258
259     // close renderer
260     closeRenderer();
261
262     // wait for thread before returning
263     finish = true;
264     t1.join();
265
266     return 0;
267 }
268
269
270 void createObjects(std::vector<std::shared_ptr<Wall>>& walls,
271     std::shared_ptr<Wall>& piston, std::shared_ptr<Wall>& bottom,
```

```cpp
                std::vector<std::shared_ptr<Ball>>& balls)
{
    // create walls
    for (int nw = 0; nw < 5; nw++)
    {
        walls.push_back(std::make_shared<Wall>());
    }

    // lateral walls
    walls.at(0)->setPosition(cylinder_center_position_x - cylinder_width / 2,
        cylinder_center_position_y);
    walls.at(0)->setSize(wall_width, cylinder_height + wall_width);
    walls.at(0)->setWallType(WallType::lateral);

    walls.at(1)->setPosition(cylinder_center_position_x + cylinder_width / 2,
        cylinder_center_position_y);
    walls.at(1)->setSize(wall_width, cylinder_height + wall_width);
    walls.at(1)->setWallType(WallType::lateral);

    // piston, cover and bottom walls
    walls.at(2)->setPosition(cylinder_center_position_x,
        cylinder_center_position_y - cylinder_height / 2);
    walls.at(2)->setSize(cylinder_width - wall_width, wall_width);
    walls.at(2)->setWallType(WallType::piston);

    walls.at(3)->setPosition(cylinder_center_position_x,
        cylinder_center_position_y + cylinder_height / 2);
    walls.at(3)->setSize(cylinder_width - wall_width, wall_width);
    walls.at(3)->setWallType(WallType::bottom);
    // create reference to piston
    piston = walls.at(2);
    piston->setMass(piston_mass);

    // create reference to bottom
    bottom = walls.at(3);
    bottom->setHeat(bottom_temp_min);

    // create cells into the cylinder
    int nCells = 0;         // calc number of cells

    int nRows, nCols;
    double totalArea, filedArea, percentFiled;

    percentFiled = 0.0;
    nRows = nCols = 0;


    for (int nc = 1; nc <= nballs; nc++)
    {
        int nr = nballs / nc;
        if (double(nc) * double(nr) < nballs) { nr += 1; }

        totalArea = (screen_height * percent_height) *
            (screen_width * percent_width);
```

```cpp
327        if ((screen_width * percent_width) / nc >
328                (screen_height * percent_height) / nr) {
329            filedArea = pow(((screen_height * percent_height) / nr) *
330                0.50, 2.0) * 3.14 * nballs;
331        }
332        else {
333            filedArea = pow(((screen_width * percent_width) / nc) *
334                0.50, 2.0) * 3.14 * nballs;
335        }
336
337        if (filedArea/totalArea > percentFiled) {
338            percentFiled = filedArea / totalArea;
339            nRows = nr;
340            nCols = nc;
341            nCells = nCols * nRows;
342        }
343
344    }
345
346    struct Cell {
347        double x, y;
348    };
349
350    std::vector<Cell> places;
351    double inicX, inicY, aux;
352    walls.at(0)->getPosition(inicX, aux);
353    inicX += wall_width * 0.5;
354    walls.at(2)->getPosition(aux, inicY);
355    inicY += wall_width * 0.5;
356
357    for (int nc = 0; nc < nCells; nc++)
358    {
359        Cell cell;
360        cell.x = (inicX)+(nc % nCols) * ((cylinder_width - wall_width) / nCols) +
361            ((cylinder_width - wall_width) / nCols) / 2.0;
362        cell.y = (inicY)+(nc / nCols) * ((cylinder_height - wall_width) / nRows) +
363            ((cylinder_height - wall_width) / nRows) / 2.0;
364        places.push_back(cell);
365    }
366
367    // create balls in the cells
368    for (int nb = 0; nb < nballs; nb++)
369    {
370        balls.push_back(std::make_shared<Ball>());
371        balls.at(nb)->setPosition(places.at(nb).x, places.at(nb).y);
372
373        // prevent ball size overflow
374        if (nCols * 2.0 * ball_radius > cylinder_width * 0.98) {
375            balls.at(nb)->setRadius(cylinder_width * 0.98 / nCols / 2.0);
376        }
377        else {
378            balls.at(nb)->setRadius(ball_radius);
379        }
380
381        balls.at(nb)->setRandomDirection(ball_speed);
```

```cpp
382            balls.at(nb)->setMass(ball_mass);
383            balls.at(nb)->setGravity(ball_gravity);
384            balls.at(nb)->setG(ball_G * G_mult);
385            balls.at(nb)->setGasMode((gas_mode > 0));
386            balls.at(nb)->setCoefRestitution(coef_rest);
387        }
388
389        // set a reference to other balls and walls into each ball
390        for (auto ball : balls)
391        {
392            ball->setBalls(balls);
393            ball->setWalls(walls);
394        }
395    }
396
397    bool initRenderer()
398    {
399        // Initialization flag
400        bool success = true;
401
402        // Initialize SDL
403        if (SDL_Init(SDL_INIT_VIDEO) < 0)
404        {
405            std::cout << "SDL could not initialize! SDL Error: " << SDL_GetError() <<
406                std::endl;
407            success = false;
408        }
409        else
410        {
411            // Create window
412            gWindow = std::shared_ptr<SDL_Window>
413                (SDL_CreateWindow("Collisions of Multiple Balls Simulation",
414                    SDL_WINDOWPOS_UNDEFINED, SDL_WINDOWPOS_UNDEFINED,
415                    int(screen_width * zoom_factor), int(screen_height * zoom_factor),
416                    SDL_WINDOW_SHOWN), SDL_DestroyWindow);
417            if (gWindow == nullptr)
418            {
419                std::cout << "Window could not be created! SDL Error: " << SDL_GetError() <<
420                    std::endl;
421                success = false;
422            }
423            else
424            {
425                // Create vsynced renderer for window
426                gRenderer = std::shared_ptr<SDL_Renderer>
427                    (SDL_CreateRenderer(gWindow.get(),
428                        -1, SDL_RENDERER_ACCELERATED | SDL_RENDERER_PRESENTVSYNC),
429                        SDL_DestroyRenderer);
430                if (gRenderer == NULL) {
431                    std::cout << "Renderer could not be created! SDL Error: " <<
432                        SDL_GetError() << std::endl;
433                    success = false;
434                }
435                else
436                {
```

```cpp
                    // Initialize renderer color
                    SDL_SetRenderDrawColor(gRenderer.get(), 0xFF, 0xFF, 0xFF, 0xFF);
                }
            }

        }

        return success;
}

void closeRenderer() {
    // Quit SDL subsystems
    SDL_Quit();
}

void drawCircle(std::shared_ptr<SDL_Renderer> renderer,
                int32_t centreX, int32_t centreY, int32_t radius)
{
    const int32_t diameter = (radius * 2);

    int32_t x = (radius - 1);
    int32_t y = 0;
    int32_t tx = 1;
    int32_t ty = 1;
    int32_t error = (tx - diameter);

    while (x >= y)
    {
        //  Each of the following renders an octant of the circle
        SDL_RenderDrawPoint(renderer.get(), centreX + x, centreY - y);
        SDL_RenderDrawPoint(renderer.get(), centreX + x, centreY + y);
        SDL_RenderDrawPoint(renderer.get(), centreX - x, centreY - y);
        SDL_RenderDrawPoint(renderer.get(), centreX - x, centreY + y);
        SDL_RenderDrawPoint(renderer.get(), centreX + y, centreY - x);
        SDL_RenderDrawPoint(renderer.get(), centreX + y, centreY + x);
        SDL_RenderDrawPoint(renderer.get(), centreX - y, centreY - x);
        SDL_RenderDrawPoint(renderer.get(), centreX - y, centreY + x);

        if (error <= 0)
        {
            ++y;
            error += ty;
            ty += 2;
        }

        if (error > 0)
        {
            --x;
            tx += 2;
            error += (tx - diameter);
        }
    }
}

void renderBall(std::shared_ptr<Ball> ball)
```

```cpp
492    {
493        double x, y, r;
494        int info_stage;
495
496        ball->getPosition(x, y);
497        r = ball->getRadius();
498        info_stage = ball->getInfoStage();
499
500        x = x * zoom_factor;
501        y = y * zoom_factor;
502        r = r * zoom_factor;
503
504        if (r < 1) r = 1;   // prevent the no plotting of smaller balls
505
506        if (x < 0) return;
507
508        // DONE: adjust colors according to "info" stage
509        if (background_color != 1) {
510            if (info_stage == 0) {
511                SDL_SetRenderDrawColor(gRenderer.get(), 0xFF, 0xFF, 0xFF, 0xFF);
512            }
513            else if (info_stage == 1) {
514                SDL_SetRenderDrawColor(gRenderer.get(), 0xFF, 0x20, 0x20, 0xFF);
515            }
516            else if (info_stage == 2) {
517                SDL_SetRenderDrawColor(gRenderer.get(), 0x20, 0xAB, 0x20, 0xFF);
518            }
519
520        }
521        else {
522            if (info_stage == 0) {
523                SDL_SetRenderDrawColor(gRenderer.get(), 0x00, 0x00, 0x00, 0xFF);
524            }
525            else if (info_stage == 1) {
526                SDL_SetRenderDrawColor(gRenderer.get(), 0xFF, 0x20, 0x20, 0xFF);
527            }
528            else if (info_stage == 2) {
529                SDL_SetRenderDrawColor(gRenderer.get(), 0x20, 0xAB, 0x20, 0xFF);
530            }
531        }
532
533        drawCircle(gRenderer, (int32_t) x, (int32_t) y, (int32_t) r);
534
535    }
536
537    void renderWalls(std::vector<std::shared_ptr<Wall>> walls)
538    {
539        for (auto wall : walls) {
540
541            // set the rectangle
542            SDL_Rect rect;
543            double x, y, w, h;
544            wall->getPosition(x, y);
545            wall->getSize(w, h);
546
```

```cpp
            x = x * zoom_factor;
            y = y * zoom_factor;
            w = w * zoom_factor;
            h = h * zoom_factor;

            if (x < 0) continue;

            rect.x = int (x - w / 2);
            rect.y = int (y - h / 2);
            rect.w = int (w);
            rect.h = int (h);

            switch (wall->getWallType())
            {
                case WallType::lateral:
                    //SDL_SetRenderDrawColor(gRenderer.get(), 0x00, 0x00, 0x00, 0xFF);
                    SDL_SetRenderDrawColor(gRenderer.get(), 0xAF, 0xAF, 0xAF, 0xFF);
                    break;
                case WallType::piston:
                    SDL_SetRenderDrawColor(gRenderer.get(), 0x00, 0x00, 0xFF, 0xFF);
                    break;
                case WallType::bottom:
                    double k = (wall->getHeat() - bottom_temp_min) /
                        (bottom_temp_max + 0.001);
                    double kMin = bottom_temp_min / (bottom_temp_max + 0.001);
                    uint8_t red = uint8_t(0xFF * 0.60 + (0xFF * kMin + 0xFF * k) * 0.40);
                    SDL_SetRenderDrawColor(gRenderer.get(), red, 0x00, 0x00, 0xFF);
                    break;
            }

            SDL_RenderDrawRect(gRenderer.get(), &rect);
        }
    }


    bool loadParametersFromFile()
    {

        struct Reading {
            std::string name;
            double value;
        };

        std::cout << "Loading parameters file...\n" << std::endl;
        std::cout << "Please enter input <path>/<filename>: [C:/tmp/Parameters.txt]";

        std::string iname;
        std::getline(std::cin, iname);

        if (iname.empty()) {
            iname = "C:/tmp/Parameters.txt";
        }

        // the input stream
        std::ifstream ist{ iname };
```

```cpp
602
603     if (!ist)
604     {
605         std::cout << "\nCan't open input file " << iname << std::endl;
606         return false;
607     }
608
609     if (ist)
610     {
611         std::cout << "Reading the file " << iname << " ...\n" << std::endl;
612     }
613
614     // it will store the data
615     std::vector<Reading> parameters;
616
617     // reading from file
618     while (ist) {
619         std::string name{};
620         double value{};
621         ist >> name >> value;
622         if (ist) {
623             parameters.push_back(Reading{ name, value });
624         }
625     }
626
627     // test the data
628     if (parameters.size() != 38)
629         return false;
630
631     // load in memory
632     for (auto parameter : parameters)
633     {
634         if (parameter.name == "GAS_MODE") gas_mode = parameter.value;
635
636         if (parameter.name == "NBALLS") nballs = int(parameter.value);
637         if (parameter.name == "BALL_RADIUS") ball_radius = parameter.value;
638         if (parameter.name == "BALL_SPEED") ball_speed = parameter.value;
639         if (parameter.name == "BALL_MASS") ball_mass = parameter.value;
640         if (parameter.name == "BALL_GRAVITY") ball_gravity = parameter.value;
641         if (parameter.name == "BALL_G") ball_G = parameter.value;
642         if (parameter.name == "PUSH_PULL") push_pull = int(parameter.value);
643         if (parameter.name == "COEF_RESTITUTION") coef_rest = parameter.value;
644
645         if (parameter.name == "IS_TESTING") is_testing = int(parameter.value);
646         // DONE: load the is_info_simulation global variable
647         if (parameter.name == "IS_INFO_SIMULATION") is_info_simulation =
648             int(parameter.value);
649         // DONE: load the duration of intermediarie stage global variable
650         if (parameter.name == "INTER_PERIOD") inter_period = parameter.value;
651
652         if (parameter.name == "BALL0_SPEED") ball0_speed = parameter.value;
653         if (parameter.name == "BALL0_VEL_ANGLE") ball0_vel_angle = parameter.value;
654
655         if (parameter.name == "BALL0_X") ball0_x = parameter.value;
656         if (parameter.name == "BALL0_Y") ball0_y = parameter.value;
```

```cpp
        if (parameter.name == "BALL0_RADIUS") ball0_radius = parameter.value;
        if (parameter.name == "BALL0_MASS") ball0_mass = parameter.value;

        if (parameter.name == "BALL0_TIME") ball0_time = parameter.value;
        if (parameter.name == "BALL0_DELTA_SPEED") ball0_delta_speed = parameter.value;
        if (parameter.name == "BALL0_DELTA_ANGLE") ball0_delta_angle = parameter.value;

        if (parameter.name == "BALL1_SPEED") ball1_speed = parameter.value;
        if (parameter.name == "BALL1_VEL_ANGLE") ball1_vel_angle = parameter.value;
        if (parameter.name == "BALL1_X") ball1_x = parameter.value;
        if (parameter.name == "BALL1_Y") ball1_y = parameter.value;
        if (parameter.name == "BALL1_RADIUS") ball1_radius = parameter.value;
        if (parameter.name == "BALL1_MASS") ball1_mass = parameter.value;

        if (parameter.name == "PISTON_MASS") piston_mass = parameter.value;
        if (parameter.name == "PISTON_GRAVITY") piston_gravity = parameter.value;

        if (parameter.name == "BOTTOM_TEMP_MIN") bottom_temp_min = parameter.value;
        if (parameter.name == "BOTTOM_TEMP_MAX") bottom_temp_max = parameter.value;

        if (parameter.name == "BACKGROUND") background_color = int(parameter.value);

        if (parameter.name == "SCREEN_WIDTH") screen_width = parameter.value;
        if (parameter.name == "PERCENT_WIDTH") percent_width = parameter.value;

        if (parameter.name == "SCREEN_HEIGHT") screen_height = parameter.value;
        if (parameter.name == "PERCENT_HEIGHT") percent_height = parameter.value;

        if (parameter.name == "WALL_WIDTH") wall_width = parameter.value;

        if (parameter.name == "ZOOM_FACTOR") zoom_factor = parameter.value;

        cylinder_center_position_x = screen_width / 2;
        cylinder_center_position_y = screen_height / 2;
        cylinder_width = screen_width * percent_width;
        cylinder_height = screen_height * percent_height;

    }

    return true;
}

void printParameters()
{
    std::cout << "GAS_MODE " << gas_mode << std::endl;

    std::cout << "NBALLS " << nballs << std::endl;
    std::cout << "BALL_RADIUS " << ball_radius << std::endl;
    std::cout << "BALL_SPEED " << ball_speed << std::endl;
    std::cout << "BALL_MASS " << ball_mass << std::endl;
    std::cout << "BALL_GRAVITY " << ball_gravity << std::endl;
    std::cout << "BALL_G " << ball_G << std::endl;
    std::cout << "PUSH_PULL " << push_pull << std::endl;
    std::cout << "COEF_RESTITUTION " << coef_rest << std::endl << std::endl;
```

```cpp
        std::cout << "IS_TESTING " << is_testing << std::endl;
        // DONE: print the is_info_simulation global variable
        std::cout << "IS_INFO_SIMULATION " << is_info_simulation << std::endl;
        // DONE: print the duration of intermediarie stage global variable
        std::cout << "INTER_PERIOD " << std::fixed << std::setprecision(1) << inter_period
            << std::endl << std::endl << std::defaultfloat << std::setprecision(6);

        std::cout << "BALL0_SPEED " << ball0_speed << std::endl;
        std::cout << "BALL0_VEL_ANGLE " << ball0_vel_angle << std::endl;

        std::cout << "BALL0_X " << ball0_x << std::endl;
        std::cout << "BALL0_Y " << ball0_y << std::endl;
        std::cout << "BALL0_RADIUS " << ball0_radius << std::endl;
        std::cout << "BALL0_MASS " << ball0_mass << std::endl << std::endl;

        std::cout << "BALL0_TIME " << ball0_time << std::endl;
        std::cout << "BALL0_DELTA_SPEED " << ball0_delta_speed << std::endl;
        std::cout << "BALL0_DELTA_ANGLE " << ball0_delta_angle << std::endl << std::endl;

        std::cout << "BALL1_SPEED " << ball1_speed << std::endl;
        std::cout << "BALL1_VEL_ANGLE " << ball1_vel_angle << std::endl;
        std::cout << "BALL1_X " << ball1_x << std::endl;
        std::cout << "BALL1_Y " << ball1_y << std::endl;
        std::cout << "BALL1_RADIUS " << ball1_radius << std::endl;
        std::cout << "BALL1_MASS " << ball1_mass << std::endl << std::endl;

        std::cout << "PISTON_MASS " << piston_mass << std::endl;
        std::cout << "PISTON_GRAVITY " << piston_gravity << std::endl << std::endl;

        std::cout << "BOTTOM_TEMP_MIN " << bottom_temp_min << std::endl;
        std::cout << "BOTTOM_TEMP_MAX " << bottom_temp_max << std::endl << std::endl;

        std::cout << "BACKGROUND " << background_color << std::endl;

        std::cout << "SCREEN_WIDTH " << screen_width << std::endl;
        std::cout << "PERCENT_WIDTH " << percent_width << std::endl;

        std::cout << "SCREEN_HEIGHT " << screen_height << std::endl;
        std::cout << "PERCENT_HEIGHT " << percent_height << std::endl;

        std::cout << "WALL_WIDTH " << wall_width << std::endl;

        std::cout << "ZOOM_FACTOR " << zoom_factor << std::endl;

}


bool chooseSimulations()
{

        // DONE: create option for a "info" simmulation
        std::cout << "\n";
        std::cout << "\tPlease, choose one example or read parameters from file:" <<
            std::endl;
        std::cout << "\n";
```

```cpp
        std::cout << "\t[1] Three balls. (default)" << std::endl;
        std::cout << "\t[2] One ball at rest. Piston with gravity." << std::endl;
        std::cout << "\t[3] Eight balls at rest. Piston with gravity." << std::endl;
        std::cout << "\t[4] Fifty balls (gas simulation approximation)." <<
            " Piston with gravity." << std::endl;
        std::cout << "\t[5] Planet and Satellite." << std::endl;
        std::cout << "\t[6] A Fictional Universe." << std::endl;
        std::cout <<"\t[7] Five balls info propagation (intermediate period 20s)."<<std::endl;
        std::cout <<"\t[8] Fifty balls info propagation (intermediate period 7s)."<<std::endl;
        std::cout << "\t[9] Fifty balls info propagation (1/2 speed)." << std::endl;
        std::cout << "\t[10] Load parameters from file." << std::endl;
        std::cout << "\n";

        std::string input;
        std::cout << "\n\tOption: ";
        std::getline(std::cin, input);

        int menuOption = 1;

        if (!input.empty())
        {
            menuOption = stoi(input);
        }

        switch (menuOption)
        {
        case 1:
            // Simulation mode
            gas_mode = 0;

            // Balls
            nballs = 3;               // 100 max approx
            ball_radius = 20;         // max 0.5 * WALL_WIDTH approx
            ball_speed = 60;          // pixels/s (SPPED < RADIUS * 200 max approx)
            ball_mass = 0.1;          // 0.01 * piston_mass min approx
            ball_gravity = 0;         // if zero, simulate gas

            // Piston
            piston_mass = 10.0;
            piston_gravity = 0.0;     // if zero, piston stops
            break;

        case 2:
            // Simulation mode
            gas_mode = 0;

            // Balls
            nballs = 1;               // 100 max approx
            ball_radius = 20;         // max 0.5 * WALL_WIDTH approx
            ball_speed = 0;           // pixels/s (SPPED < RADIUS * 200 max approx)
            ball_mass = 0.2;          // 0.01 * piston_mass min approx
            ball_gravity = 0;         // if zero, simulate gas

            // Piston
            piston_mass = 10.0;
```

```cpp
822            piston_gravity = 10.0;    // if zero, piston stops
823            break;
824
825        case 3:
826            // Simulation mode
827            gas_mode = 0;
828
829            // Balls
830            nballs = 8;                // 100 max approx
831            ball_radius = 8;           // max 0.5 * WALL_WIDTH approx
832            ball_speed = 0;            // pixels/s (SPPED < RADIUS * 200 max approx)
833            ball_mass = 0.2;           // 0.01 * piston_mass min approx
834            ball_gravity = 0;          // if zero, simulate gas
835
836            // Piston
837            piston_mass = 10.0;
838            piston_gravity = 10.0;    // if zero, piston stops
839            break;
840
841        case 4:
842            // Simulation mode
843            gas_mode = 1;
844
845            // Balls
846            nballs = 50;               // 100 max approx
847            ball_radius = 4;           // max 0.5 * WALL_WIDTH approx
848            ball_speed = 60;           // pixels/s (SPPED < RADIUS * 200 max approx)
849            ball_mass = 0.1;           // 0.01 * piston_mass min approx
850            ball_gravity = 0;          // if zero, simulate gas
851
852            // Piston
853            piston_mass = 10.0;
854            piston_gravity = 10.0;    // if zero, piston stops
855            std::cout << "\n\tPlease, click on cylinder and increase energy" <<
856                " with '>' right key." << std::endl;
857            break;
858
859        case 5:
860            // Simulation mode
861            gas_mode = 0;
862            is_testing = 1;
863
864            // Balls
865            nballs = 2;                // 100 max approx
866            ball_radius = 8;           // max 0.5 * WALL_WIDTH approx
867            ball_G = 1.0;
868            push_pull = 1;
869            coef_rest = 1.0;
870
871            ball0_speed = 100.0;
872            ball0_vel_angle = 0;
873            ball0_x = 600;
874            ball0_y = 100;
875            ball0_radius = -1;
876            ball0_mass = 1e-6;
```

```
877
878            ball0_delta_speed = 1e-6;    // for turning-on the printing of orbit
879
880            ball1_speed = 0.0;
881            ball1_vel_angle = 0;
882            ball1_x = 600;
883            ball1_y = 600;
884            ball1_radius = 50;
885            ball1_mass = 50.0;
886
887            // Piston
888            piston_mass = 1e10;
889            piston_gravity = 0.0;    // if zero, piston stops
890
891            // Screen
892            background_color = 1;
893            screen_width = 1200;
894            percent_width = 0.90;
895            screen_height = 1200;
896            percent_height = 0.90;
897            wall_width = 20;
898            zoom_factor = 0.50;
899            break;
900
901        case 6:
902            // Simulation mode
903            gas_mode = 0;
904            is_testing = 0;
905
906            // Balls
907            nballs = 63;                // 100 max approx
908            ball_radius = 5;            // max 0.5 * WALL_WIDTH approx
909            ball_speed = 0;
910            ball_mass = 3.0;
911            ball_gravity = 0.0;
912            ball_G = 1.0;
913            push_pull = 0;
914            coef_rest = 0.85;
915
916            // Piston
917            piston_mass = 1e10;
918            piston_gravity = 0.0;    // if zero, piston stops
919
920            // Screen
921            background_color = 0;
922            screen_width = 4200;
923            percent_width = 0.90;
924            screen_height = 2800;
925            percent_height = 0.90;
926            wall_width = 100;
927            zoom_factor = 0.30;
928            break;
929
930        // DONE: create a small "info" simulation for testing
931        case 7:
```

```cpp
932                    // Simulation mode
933                    is_info_simulation = 1;
934                    inter_period = 20.0;
935                    gas_mode = 0;
936
937                    // Balls
938                    nballs = 5;                  // 100 max approx
939                    ball_radius = 20;             // max 0.5 * WALL_WIDTH approx
940                    ball_speed = 60;             // pixels/s (SPPED < RADIUS * 200 max approx)
941                    ball_mass = 0.1;             // 0.01 * piston_mass min approx
942                    ball_gravity = 0;            // if zero, simulate gas
943
944                    // Piston
945                    piston_mass = 10.0;
946                    piston_gravity = 0.0;        // if zero, piston stops
947
948                    // Screen
949                    screen_width = 480;
950                    percent_width = 0.90;
951                    screen_height = 480;
952                    percent_height = 0.90;
953                    wall_width = 20;
954                    zoom_factor = 1.0;
955                    break;
956
957            // DONE: create option for a "info" simmulation
958            case 8:
959                    // Simulation mode
960                    is_info_simulation = 1;
961                    inter_period = 7.0;
962                    gas_mode = 0;
963
964                    // Balls
965                    nballs = 50;                 // 100 max approx
966                    ball_radius = 4;             // max 0.5 * WALL_WIDTH approx
967                    ball_speed = 60;             // pixels/s (SPPED < RADIUS * 200 max approx)
968                    ball_mass = 0.1;             // 0.01 * piston_mass min approx
969                    ball_gravity = 0;            // if zero, simulate gas
970
971                    // Piston
972                    piston_mass = 10.0;
973                    piston_gravity = 0.0;        // if zero, piston stops
974
975                    // Screen
976                    screen_width = 480;
977                    percent_width = 0.90;
978                    screen_height = 480;
979                    percent_height = 0.90;
980                    wall_width = 20;
981                    zoom_factor = 1.0;
982                    break;
983
984            // DONE: create option for a "info" simmulation
985            case 9:
986                    // Simulation mode
```

```cpp
 987            is_info_simulation = 1;
 988            inter_period = 7.0;
 989            gas_mode = 0;
 990
 991            // Balls
 992            nballs = 50;                // 100 max approx
 993            ball_radius = 4;            // max 0.5 * WALL_WIDTH approx
 994            ball_speed = 30;            // pixels/s (SPPED < RADIUS * 200 max approx)
 995            ball_mass = 0.1;            // 0.01 * piston_mass min approx
 996            ball_gravity = 0;           // if zero, simulate gas
 997
 998            // Piston
 999            piston_mass = 10.0;
1000            piston_gravity = 0.0;       // if zero, piston stops
1001
1002            // Screen
1003            screen_width = 480;
1004            percent_width = 0.90;
1005            screen_height = 480;
1006            percent_height = 0.90;
1007            wall_width = 20;
1008            zoom_factor = 1.0;
1009            break;
1010
1011        case 10:
1012            if (!loadParametersFromFile())
1013            {
1014                std::cout << "\tCan not load the parameters file." << std::endl;
1015                std::cout << "\tPlease, verify if the file is at same directory " <<
1016                    "of the executable (.exe) " <<
1017                    "and if it has all the parameters." << std::endl;
1018                std::cout << "\tContinue with the default? [y]" << std::endl;
1019                std::string tc;
1020                std::getline(std::cin, tc);
1021                if (tc.empty()) {
1022                    tc = "y";
1023                }
1024                if (tc == "y")
1025                {
1026                    // Simulation mode
1027                    gas_mode = 0;
1028                    // Ball
1029                    nballs = 3;             // 100 max approx
1030                    ball_radius = 20;       // max 0.5 * WALL_WIDTH approx
1031                    ball_speed = 60;        // pixels/s (SPPED < RADIUS * 200 max approx)
1032                    ball_mass = 0.1;        // 0.01 * piston_mass min approx
1033                    ball_gravity = 0;       // if zero, simulate gas
1034                    // Piston
1035                    piston_mass = 10.0;
1036                    piston_gravity = 0.0;   // if zero, piston stops
1037                    break;
1038                }
1039
1040                return false;
1041            }
```

```cpp
1042            break;
1043
1044        default:
1045            // Simulation mode
1046            gas_mode = 0;
1047            // Ball
1048            nballs = 3;                 // 100 max approx
1049            ball_radius = 20;           // max 0.5 * WALL_WIDTH approx
1050            ball_speed = 60;            // pixels/s (SPPED < RADIUS * 200 max approx)
1051            ball_mass = 0.1;            // 0.01 * piston_mass min approx
1052            ball_gravity = 0;           // if zero, simulate gas
1053            // Piston
1054            piston_mass = 100.0;
1055            piston_gravity = 0.0;       // if zero, piston stops
1056            break;
1057        }
1058
1059    cylinder_center_position_x = screen_width / 2;
1060    cylinder_center_position_y = screen_height / 2;
1061    cylinder_width = screen_width * percent_width;
1062    cylinder_height = screen_height * percent_height;
1063
1064    std::cout << "\nPlease, verify the simulation parameters:\n" << std::endl;
1065    printParameters();
1066
1067    std::cout << "\nPress enter to continue..." << std::endl;
1068    std::cin.ignore();
1069
1070    return true;
1071    }
1072
```

This file will have 38 parameters. All of them must be present because the program verifies its integrity by making a simple test by counting the parameters.

```
 1    GAS_MODE  0
 2    NBALLS  50
 3    BALL_RADIUS  4
 4    BALL_SPEED  60
 5    BALL_MASS  1.0
 6    BALL_GRAVITY  0
 7    BALL_G 0
 8    PUSH_PULL 1
 9    COEF_RESTITUTION 1.0
10
11    IS_TESTING  0
12    IS_INFO_SIMULATION 1
13    INTER_PERIOD 3.0
14
15    BALL0_SPEED 0.0
16    BALL0_VEL_ANGLE  0
17    BALL0_X -1
18    BALL0_Y -1
19    BALL0_RADIUS -1
20    BALL0_MASS -1
21
22    BALL0_TIME 0
23    BALL0_DELTA_SPEED 0
24    BALL0_DELTA_ANGLE 0
25
26    BALL1_SPEED  0
27    BALL1_VEL_ANGLE  0
28    BALL1_X -1
29    BALL1_Y -1
30    BALL1_RADIUS -1
31    BALL1_MASS -1
32
33    PISTON_MASS  1e10
34    PISTON_GRAVITY  0.0
35
36    BOTTOM_TEMP_MIN  0.0
37    BOTTOM_TEMP_MAX  100.0
38
39    BACKGROUND 0
40    SCREEN_WIDTH 480
41    PERCENT_WIDTH 0.90
42    SCREEN_HEIGHT 480
43    PERCENT_HEIGHT 0.90
44    WALL_WIDTH 20
45    ZOOM_FACTOR 1.00
```

CMakeLists.txt

```cmake
1    cmake_minimum_required (VERSION 3.5)
2
3    add_definitions(-std=c++17)
4
5    set(CXX_FLAGS, "-Wall")
6    set(CMAKE_CXX_FLAGS, "${CXX_FLAGS}")
7
8    project(MbcsProjectCmake)
9
10   set(CMAKE_MODULE_PATH ${CMAKE_MODULE_PATH} "${CMAKE_SOURCE_DIR}/cmake/")
11
12   find_package(SDL2 REQUIRED)
13   include_directories(${SDL2_INCLUDE_DIRS} src)
14
15   find_package(Threads)
16
17   add_executable(MbcsProjectCmake "src/Main.cpp" "src/CylinderObject.cpp"
18                  "src/Wall.cpp" "src/Ball.cpp" "src/Piston.cpp")
19   string(STRIP "${SDL2_LIBRARIES}" SDL2_LIBRARIES)
20   target_link_libraries(MbcsProjectCmake ${CMAKE_THREAD_LIBS_INIT} ${SDL2_LIBRARIES} )
```